FORT WORTH

PUBLIC LIBRARY

And MetroPac Libraries

COOKING

WITH THE

ORIGINAL

SEARCH ENGINE

LIBRARIES
HAVE IT ALL

COOKING WITH THE ORIGINAL SEARCH ENGINE
Copyright © 2001 by
Fort Worth Public Library
All Staff Association
Fort Worth, Texas

www.fortworthlibrary.org

A Book of Favorite Recipes: 641.5 and *641.5 Too:
Cooking in the Stacks,* previously published by the Fort Worth
Public Library, are out of print but are available on loan at
your local library through the Inter-Library Loan Department.

All photographs courtesy of Archives of Fort Worth
Public Library

This cookbook is a collection of favorite recipes,
which are not necessarily original recipes.
Liberties have been taken to ensure consistency of form.

Library of Congress Catalog Number: 2001 126562
ISBN: 0-9710166-0-7

Edited, Designed, and Manufactured by Favorite Recipes® Press
An imprint of

FRP™

P.O. Box 305142, Nashville, Tennessee 37230
800-358-0560

Manufactured in the United States of America
First Printing: 2001   6,000 copies

TO ORDER ADDITIONAL COPIES,
please contact Cookbook Committee
Fort Worth Public Library All Staff Association
Central Library
500 W. 3rd Street
Fort Worth, Texas 76102
Price is $24.95, which includes shipping and handling.

Contents

Introduction

From a military post on the Trinity River to a booming western town, Fort Worth became a city known to many as Cowtown. This is where the West began for many first settlers, and the City has proudly retained that title for the citizens of today.

Fort Worth Public Library is celebrating 100 years (1901-2001) of giving quality service to the citizens of Fort Worth. *The Original Search Engine* is the library's logo for this century of books to the Internet. The All Staff Association theme is Cooking with the Original Search Engine, as Libraries have it All! The seed of thought for a public library started with a group of women in 1892. In 1901, Carnegie Public Library was opened in October with 6,907 volumes. The Library included a United States Depository for government documents and the Fort Worth Museum of Art.

The Carnegie Library gave way to a new building on the same site in June of 1939. The 915 Throckmorton Street Library was completed and built with the aid of Public Works Administration funds. When another larger library was needed, a new building on Taylor between 2nd and 3rd was planned. Despite receiving voter approval in 1972, it was delayed by litigation until 1975. The heirs of Sarah Gray Jennings sued the City to regain ownership of the property on Throckmorton since it was no longer used for a library or for educational purposes. The loss of funds due to double-digit inflation resulted in an underground building as the only alternative. The building was completed in 1978. The underground library served Fort Worth well but was plagued by leaks until an additional construction was done in 1993. The Fort Worth Foundation was founded this year and played a major role in raising the necessary funds to accomplish this capital improvement task.

Today the Fort Worth Public Library has a material collection of 2.2 million with a circulation of 5 million items. Library card holders currently number 280,000. The Fort Worth Public Library has a regional approach to providing service to the citizens with two regional libraries, twelve branches, and a Central Library.

The All Staff Association is an avenue to assist in increasing staff morale, increase services, and be proactive in communications, with a unique relationship with staff and administrators. The All Staff Association provides several off-site activities for staff and families to attend. The annual workshop provides the staff the opportunity to gather as a unit to create work and social relationships.

The MetroPac Libraries are a group of surrounding cities that united to increase their service area for their patrons. In 1993, Keller Public Library was the first to sign the inter-local agreement with Fort Worth Public Library. Fort Worth Public Library and the MetroPacs have entered into the new century with an agreement in 1998 for resource sharing for the citizens. The cities of Texas involved are Fort Worth, Haltom City, Keller, Richland Hills, and Watauga.

Each Library has groups as Friends of the Library or a Library Foundation that have helped them achieve such goals. Fort Worth Library is the distinguished recipient of both groups. Throughout this cookbook we hope you will enjoy reading the history and fun activities the Fort Worth Public Library and the MetroPac Libraries have offered their citizens.

Bookmobile service was initiated under the direction of Joseph Ibbotson in 1948. At that time, the Bookmobile made twenty-eight stops within the Fort Worth city limits.

In Appreciation

The cover picture depicts the original Carnegie Public Library of Fort Worth, Texas. The Classical style red brick building was opened to the public in October 1901.

One hundred years later, the Fort Worth Public Library continues its role to bring quality service to the community. Dr. Gleniece Robinson, Library Director (1999-present), states the library can provide this service by reaching out to the traditional users who come into our libraries, the virtual user, and by providing a Community Services Outreach Department. This department will include Human Services Specialists, one each for Children, Teens, Senior Citizens, and Volunteer Services. Fort Worth is known as the City "Where the West Begins."

The Cookbook Committee and the All Staff Association would like to extend our thanks to the Genealogy/Local History and Archives Department for giving us permission to use the pictures found on the cover and chapter openers. We would also like to thank Administration for their assistance. A Thank You also goes to the many individuals who donated recipes, provided history tidbits, voted on the cookbook title, and made this project a reality.

Cookbook Committee

Lynn Allen, *Chair*
Brenda Lanche, *Co-Chair*
Linda Waggener, *Co-Chair*

Leticia Alviar
Connie Barnes
Becky Deaton
Marion Edwards
Virginia M. Gonzalez

Max Hill
Betty Howe
Jo Anne Mitchell
Roberta Schenewerk
Mary Taggart Sikes

The Original Search Engine
100
FORT WORTH
PUBLIC LIBRARY
1901-2001

BEVERAGES & APPETIZERS

ap·pe·tiz·er (ap′i·tī′zər) *n.*

Food or drink served before a
meal to whet the appetite.

Shown above: Carnegie Public Library, Reference Department, 1901-1938

Berry Banana Smoothie

1 small banana, peeled, chopped
1 cup orange juice
1/4 to 1/2 cup chopped fresh
   strawberries

3 tablespoons low-fat vanilla
   yogurt

Place the banana in a sealable plastic bag or freezer container. Freeze until firm. Combine the frozen banana, orange juice, strawberries and yogurt in a blender container. Process until smooth. Pour into tall glasses. Garnish with additional fresh strawberries. Serve immediately.

Serves 1
Ellen Warthoe, Ridglea/Wedgwood Branches

Cold Grapefruit Nog

2 eggs
2 tablespoons sugar

2 cups grapefruit juice, chilled

Combine the eggs and sugar in a mixing bowl. Beat until light and fluffy. Add the grapefruit juice. Beat until blended. Pour into glasses. To avoid raw eggs that may carry salmonella, we suggest using an equivalent amount of pasteurized egg substitute.

Serves 2
Corina Escamilla, Wedgwood Branch

Lemon Tonic

1/2 cup fresh lemon juice
1/4 cup sugar

6 whole cloves
1 1/2 cups tonic water, chilled

Combine the lemon juice and sugar in a pitcher and stir until the sugar dissolves. Stir in the cloves. Add the tonic water and mix well. Pour over ice in glasses.

Serves 2
Corina Escamilla, Wedgwood Branch

Hot Orange Juice Nog

1/4 cup sugar
2 eggs

1 cup orange juice
2 cups milk, scalded

Combine the sugar and eggs in a mixing bowl. Beat until light and fluffy. Add the orange juice. Beat until blended. Stir in the milk. Pour into mugs.

Serves 4
Corina Escamilla, Wedgwood Branch

Frothy Orange Soda

1 cup orange juice
1 cup vanilla ice cream

1 cup lemon-lime soda

Combine the orange juice and ice cream in a blender container. Process until smooth. Stir in the soda. Pour into glasses. Serve immediately.

Serves 2
Sylvia Autrey, Wedgwood Branch

Sangria

This recipe is from the Casa Pacos restaurant in Madrid, Spain.

3/4 cup sugar
1/2 cup lemon juice, chilled
1/2 cup orange juice, chilled
1 1/2 (750-milliliter) bottles dry
    red wine

1 (7-ounce) bottle club soda, chilled
1/4 cup brandy
1 tray ice cubes
Apple slices

Combine the sugar, lemon juice and orange juice in a large pitcher and stir until the sugar dissolves. Add the wine, club soda and brandy and mix well. Stir in the ice cubes and apple slices. Pour into glasses. Serve immediately.

    May be prepared early in the day and stored, covered, in the refrigerator, adding the club soda, ice and apples just before serving.

Serves 6
Clark Strickland, Ella Mae Shamblee Branch

Blushing Rose Punch

2 cups cranberry juice cocktail
1½ cups fresh lemon juice
1 cup sugar
1 ice ring
2 (28-ounce) bottles ginger ale, chilled
1 quart raspberry sherbet
Lemon or lime slices

Combine the cranberry juice cocktail, lemon juice and sugar in a pitcher and mix well. Chill, covered, in the refrigerator. Pour the juice mixture over the ice ring in a punch bowl. Stir in the ginger ale. Stir in the sherbet gently. Garnish with lemon or lime slices. Ladle into punch cups.

Serves 30
Sylvia Autrey, Wedgwood Branch

Pink Champagne Punch

2 (6-ounce) cans frozen cranberry juice concentrate
2 (6-ounce) cans frozen pink lemonade concentrate
1 bottle burgundy, chilled
1 quart club soda
2 bottles pink Champagne

Combine the cranberry juice concentrate, lemonade concentrate, wine, club soda and Champagne in a punch bowl and mix well. Add the desired amount of ice cubes. Ladle into punch cups.

Serves 35
Corina Escamilla, Wedgwood Branch

Champagne (sham·PAYN)
A sparkling wine from the Champagne region in France.

Festive Punch

1 gallon lime or orange sherbet
2 (2-liter) bottles ginger ale
2 (2-liter) bottles lemon-lime soda

Let the sherbet stand at room temperature for 30 minutes to soften. Pour ½ of 1 bottle of the ginger ale gradually into a punch bowl. Add ½ of 1 bottle of the soda and mix well. Scoop large mounds of ½ gallon of the sherbet into the punch bowl.

Pour the remaining open bottle of ginger ale and open bottle of soda into the punch bowl and stir gently. Replenish with the remaining ginger ale, remaining soda and remaining sherbet.

Serves 35
Rodney Bland, Haltom City Public Library

Fruit Punch

2 oranges, sliced
2 small lemons, sliced
2 limes, sliced
1 can Hawaiian punch concentrate
2 (2-liter) bottles lemon-lime soda, chilled
1 (2-liter) bottle ginger ale, chilled

Place the orange slices, lemon slices and lime slices in the bottom of a large punch bowl. Pour the punch concentrate over the fruit. Let stand for 30 minutes. Add the soda and ginger ale and mix well. Add the desired amount of ice. Ladle into punch cups.

Serves 20 to 25
Rodney Bland, Haltom City Public Library

Celebrating the First 100 Years

On October 23, 2000, the Fort Worth Public Library announced that it had adopted "The Original Search Engine" as its centennial theme. Plans to add 100,000 new library users to its current 280,000 were unveiled as part of a multi-media campaign to highlight the many free services available. In addition, there are plans for the formation of a Speaker's Bureau, and the introduction of Community Outreach Services, bringing library services directly into the community.

(continued on page 14)

Pineapple Wine Punch

1 bottle chablis
1 (16-ounce) can pineapple juice
1 pound fresh strawberries, sliced, or
   1 (10-ounce) package frozen sliced
    strawberries

2 kiwifruit, peeled, thinly sliced
2 tablespoons brandy
12 to 15 ice cubes

Combine the wine and pineapple juice in a punch bowl. Stir in the strawberries and kiwifruit. Add the brandy and ice cubes and mix well. Ladle into punch cups.

Serves 8 to 10
Corina Escamilla, Wedgwood Branch

Barbara's Retirement Punch

Everyone knows that my favorite color is purple. My sister-in-law, Evelyn, along with my daughter Kaye, concocted this purple punch for my retirement reception.

4 cups boiling water
2 cups sugar
2 (3-ounce) packages grape gelatin
2 (64-ounce) bottles cran-grape juice
1 (12-ounce) can frozen grape juice
   concentrate

1 (12-ounce) can frozen lemonade
   concentrate
2 envelopes grape drink mix
5 (2-liter) bottles ginger ale,
   lemon-lime soda or club soda

Combine the boiling water, sugar and gelatin in a large heatproof container and stir until the sugar and gelatin dissolve. Add the cran-grape juice, grape juice concentrate, lemonade concentrate and drink mix and mix well. Freeze for up to 1 month.

To serve, allow the frozen punch mixture to stand at room temperature for 2 hours. Place the frozen mixture in a punch bowl and break into chunks with a fork. Add the ginger ale and continue breaking up the mixture until of a slushy consistency. Ladle into punch cups.

Serves 100
Barbara M. Smith, Central Library (retired)

Wedding Punch

2 (3-ounce) packages strawberry or raspberry gelatin
1 (6-ounce) can frozen lemonade concentrate
2 (6-ounce) cans frozen orange juice concentrate
1 (46-ounce) can pineapple juice
1/2 cup sugar
1 tablespoon almond extract
1 (2-liter) bottle ginger ale

Prepare the gelatin using package directions. Let stand until cool. Prepare the lemonade concentrate and orange juice concentrate using package directions, reducing the water by 1 can for each concentrate.

Combine the gelatin, lemonade, orange juice, pineapple juice, sugar and flavoring in a large freezer container and mix well. Freeze until firm. Let stand at room temperature until partially thawed. Break the frozen mixture into chunks and place in a punch bowl. Add the ginger ale and mix gently. Ladle into punch cups.

Serves 20
Cornelia Pim, Seminary South Branch

Fireside Coffee

2 cups chocolate drink mix
2 cups nondairy creamer
1 1/2 cups sugar
1 cup instant coffee granules
1 teaspoon cinnamon
1/2 teaspoon nutmeg

Combine the drink mix, nondairy creamer, sugar, coffee granules, cinnamon and nutmeg in a bowl and mix well. Spoon the coffee mixture into a jar with a tight-fitting lid. Mix 2 teaspoons of the coffee mixture with 1 cup hot water for each serving.

Serves 140
Angie Critchett, Haltom City Public Library

The First 100 Years, continued

Also, as part of the centennial celebration, details for a new 2,000-square-foot Teen Center, to be located on the lower level of the Central Library were announced. It will house magazines aimed at teenagers, internet terminals, subscription databases, and CD-ROMs.

Instant Spice Tea

I usually make this tea during the Christmas season for gifts, but some of my friends and fellow librarians partake all year round.

1 cup orange instant breakfast drink mix
1 cup sugar
1/2 cup sweetened lemon instant tea granules
1 teaspoon cinnamon
1 teaspoon ground cloves

Combine the drink mix, sugar, tea granules, cinnamon and cloves in a bowl and mix well. Spoon the tea mixture into a jar with a tight-fitting lid. Mix 3 to 4 teaspoons of the tea mixture with 6 ounces hot water for each serving.

Serves 30 to 40
Karen Brown, Central Library

Hot Sauce

1 (28-ounce) can tomatoes, drained
1 to 3 tablespoons sliced jalapeño chiles
2 teaspoons sugar
1 teaspoon garlic salt
1 teaspoon minced dried onion
1/8 teaspoon pepper

Combine the tomatoes, jalapeño chiles, sugar, garlic salt, onion and pepper in a blender container. Process just until blended. Chill, covered, for 8 to 10 hours.

Makes 2½ to 3 cups
Frances Allen, Ella Mae Shamblee Branch

Pico de Gallo

Translated, pico de gallo means the "bite from the rooster's beak." Sprinkle on melons, oranges, pears, kiwifruit, and jicama, as well as popcorn and corn on the cob.

3 tablespoons paprika
2 tablespoons ground red chiles
1 tablespoon cayenne pepper
1 tablespoon finely ground black pepper
1 tablespoon salt, or to taste

Combine the paprika, red chiles, cayenne pepper, black pepper and salt in a bowl and mix well. Spoon into a shaker. Drizzle fruit with lime juice before sprinkling with the spice mixture.

Makes ½ cup
Hilda Olson, Central Library

Broccoli Dip

1 medium onion, chopped
1 rib celery, chopped
1 (10-ounce) can cream of mushroom soup
1 (4-ounce) can mushroom pieces, drained
2 rolls garlic cheese, coarsely chopped
1 (10-ounce) package frozen chopped broccoli, cooked, drained
Worcestershire sauce to taste
Lemon juice to taste

Sauté the onion and celery in a large nonstick skillet until tender. Stir in the soup, mushroom pieces and garlic cheese. Cook over low heat until the cheese melts, stirring frequently. Add the broccoli and mix well. Stir in Worcestershire sauce and lemon juice.

Cook just until heated through, stirring frequently. Spoon the broccoli dip into a chafing dish. Serve with corn chips.

Serves 15 to 20
Cornelia Pim, Seminary South Branch

Mexican Corn Dip

2 (11-ounce) cans Mexicorn, drained
2 (4-ounce) cans chopped green chiles, drained
1 jalapeño chile, seeded, chopped
10 ounces Cheddar cheese, shredded
1 cup sour cream
½ cup mayonnaise-type salad dressing
2 tablespoons picante sauce
Garlic powder to taste

Combine the Mexicorn, green chiles, jalapeño chile, cheese, sour cream, salad dressing, picante sauce and garlic powder in a bowl and mix well. Serve with corn chips.

Serves 8 to 10
Clark Strickland, Ella Mae Shamblee Branch

Martha's Dip

1 pound ground beef
1 (10-ounce) can cream of chicken soup
1 (10-ounce) can cream of mushroom soup
1 (10-ounce) can Cheddar cheese soup
1 (10-ounce) can enchilada sauce

Brown the ground beef in a skillet, stirring until crumbly; drain. Stir in the soups and enchilada sauce and mix well. Spoon into a baking dish. Bake at 350 degrees for 30 minutes or until bubbly. Serve with Doritos or tortilla chips.

Serves 8 to 10
Martha Carter, Central Library

Oklahoma Dip

We always teased my sister about serving something called Oklahoma Dip to a bunch of native Texans. Whenever I serve this dip, it always bring a smile to my face because of all the wonderful memories of family gatherings.

2 pounds ground beef
1 pound mild or hot bulk breakfast
    sausage
1 medium or large onion, chopped
2 pounds Velveeta cheese, cubed

8 ounces Cheddar cheese, finely
    shredded
2 (10-ounce) cans tomatoes with
    green chiles

Brown the ground beef and sausage with the onion in a skillet, stirring until the ground beef and sausage are crumbly; drain. Combine the Velveeta cheese, Cheddar cheese and undrained tomatoes in a saucepan.

Cook over low heat until the cheeses melt, stirring frequently. Stir in the ground beef mixture. Cook just until heated through, stirring frequently. Spoon into a chafing dish. Serve with tortilla chips. May freeze for future use.

Serves 25 to 30
Dianne Elrod, Haltom City Public Library

Salsa al Fresco

3 tomatoes, chopped
2 serrano or jalapeño chiles, sliced
½ Anaheim chile, sliced
1 bunch green onions, sliced

4 teaspoons lemon juice
½ teaspoon salt
¼ teaspoon minced garlic
Chopped fresh cilantro to taste

Combine the tomatoes, serrano chiles, Anaheim chile, green onions, lemon juice, salt, garlic and cilantro in a bowl and mix well. Chill, covered, for 30 minutes. Serve with corn or tortilla chips.

Serves 4 to 6
Lesley Smith, Haltom City Public Library

Seven-Layer Dip

1 or 2 avocados, peeled
Lemon juice to taste
Garlic salt to taste
1 (16-ounce) can refried beans
1 cup sour cream
1 cup shredded Cheddar cheese

1 (4-ounce) can sliced black olives,
    drained
Sliced jalapeño chiles or green onions
    to taste
1 medium tomato, chopped

Mash the avocado in a bowl. Stir in lemon juice and garlic salt. Layer the beans, avocado mixture, sour cream, cheese, olives, jalapeño chiles and tomato in the order listed in a shallow dish. Chill, covered, until serving time. Serve with tortilla chips.

Serves 10 to 12
Frances Allen, Ella Mae Shamblee Branch

Shrimp Dip

1 (1-pound) package frozen deveined
    peeled shrimp
8 ounces cream cheese, softened
1 can frozen cream of shrimp soup,
    thawed
1 to 2 tablespoons grated onion

1 tablespoon lemon juice
1/8 teaspoon salt
1/8 teaspoon Tabasco sauce
1/8 teaspoon Worcestershire sauce
Mayonnaise-type salad dressing

Cook the shrimp using package directions. Drain and chop. Beat the cream cheese in a mixing bowl until smooth. Stir in the shrimp, soup, onion, lemon juice, salt, Tabasco sauce and Worcestershire sauce. Add just enough salad dressing to bind the ingredients and mix well. Chill, covered, for several hours. Serve with assorted party crackers.

Serves 8 to 10
Clark Strickland, Ella Mae Shamblee Branch

Guy Pete's Shrimp Dip

Daddy was famous for making his shrimp dip for the Texas Shrimp Association conventions or other civic functions in Brownsville, Texas and Washington, D.C. Of course, he always provided the shrimp.

2 pounds shrimp, steamed, peeled, deveined
10 green onions
8 ounces cream cheese, softened
Juice of 1 lemon

Mayonnaise to taste
Salt and pepper to taste
Worcestershire sauce to taste
Tabasco sauce to taste

Grind the shrimp and green onions coarsely in a meat grinder. Combine the shrimp mixture with the cream cheese, lemon juice, mayonnaise, salt, pepper, Worcestershire sauce and Tabasco sauce in a bowl and mix well, adding additional mayonnaise as needed for the desired consistency.

Serve with assorted party crackers and/or fresh vegetables. May substitute crab meat for the shrimp or add crab meat along with the shrimp for variety.

Serves 10 to 12
Lynn Allen, Diamond Hill/Jarvis Branch

Spinach Dip

1 (10-ounce) package frozen chopped spinach, thawed, drained
1 cup mayonnaise

1 cup sour cream
1 envelope leek soup mix
½ cup shredded mozzarella cheese

Press the excess moisture from the spinach. Combine the spinach, mayonnaise, sour cream and soup mix in a saucepan and mix well. Cook over low heat just until heated through, stirring frequently. Remove from heat. Add the cheese and stir until the cheese melts. Serve hot or cold with party bread, crackers and/or fresh vegetables.

For variety, cut the top from a round loaf of bread. Remove the center carefully, leaving a shell. Cut the bread from the center into cubes. Spoon the spinach dip into the bread shell and replace the bread top. Wrap the loaf in foil. Bake at 350 degrees for 25 minutes or until heated through. Serve with the bread cubes. May serve cold instead of hot.

Serves 6 to 8
Gena Fisher, Central Library

Grab Bag Dip

I obtained this recipe from a friend in Tehran, Iran.

2 cups mayonnaise
½ cup prepared horseradish
2 teaspoons lemon juice
2 teaspoons dry hot mustard
½ teaspoon MSG (optional)
½ teaspoon salt
Cocktail sausages

Mushroom buttons
Pickled onions
Meatballs
Steamed shrimp
Lobster meat
Black olives
Cooked chicken livers

Combine the mayonnaise, horseradish, lemon juice, dry mustard, MSG and salt in a saucepan and mix well. Cook over low heat just until heated through, stirring frequently. Spoon the horseradish sauce into a chafing dish. Add cocktail sausages, mushrooms, pickled onions, meatballs, shrimp, lobster, olives, chicken livers and/or any other interesting tidbits and mix well. Serve with wooden picks.

Serves 6 to 8
Clark Strickland, Ella Mae Shamblee Branch

Tortilla Pinwheels

8 ounces cream cheese, softened
1 (4-ounce) can chopped green chiles,
    drained
1 (4-ounce) can chopped black olives,
    drained
1 bunch green onions with tops,
    chopped

½ cup chopped pimentos
¼ cup ranch salad dressing
¼ cup picante sauce
3 or 4 (10-inch) flour tortillas

Combine the cream cheese, green chiles, olives, green onions, pimentos, salad dressing and picante sauce in a bowl and mix well. Spread 1 side of each tortilla to within ¼ inch of the edge with the cream cheese mixture. Roll to enclose the filling. Wrap each roll tightly with plastic wrap. Chill until serving time. Cut each roll into ½-inch slices.

Serves 6 to 8
Helen Leavell, Southwest Regional Library

Southwestern Appetizer Cheesecake

CRUST
2 cups finely crushed tortilla chips
5 tablespoons margarine, melted

FILLING
16 ounces cream cheese, softened
2 cups shredded Cheddar cheese
1 teaspoon chili powder
1/2 teaspoon cumin
1/2 teaspoon garlic powder
1 pound ground beef
1 (16-ounce) can refried beans

SOUR CREAM TOPPING AND GARNISH
1 1/2 cups sour cream
1 (4-ounce) can chopped green chiles, drained
Salsa
Chopped tomato
Chopped green onions
Chopped black olives
Sliced bell pepper

For the crust, combine the tortilla chips and margarine in a bowl and mix well. Press the crumb mixture over the bottom of a greased springform pan. Bake at 325 degrees for 15 minutes. Maintain the oven temperature.

For the filling, beat the cream cheese in a mixing bowl until smooth. Add the Cheddar cheese, chili powder, cumin and garlic powder. Beat until mixed. Spread the cream cheese mixture over the baked layer.

Brown the ground beef in a skillet, stirring until crumbly; drain. Stir in the refried beans. Spoon the ground beef mixture over the cream cheese layer. Bake for 1 hour. Cool in pan on a wire rack.

For the topping, combine the sour cream and green chiles in a bowl and mix well. Spread over the top of the cheesecake. Garnish with salsa, chopped tomato, chopped green onions, olives and/or sliced bell pepper. The cheesecake may be sliced and served as is or served with party crackers or tortilla chips. The flavor is best if served warm or at room temperature.

Serves 20
Roberta Schenewerk, Central Library

Tortilla (tohr·TEE·yuh)
Unleavened Mexican bread made from corn flour (masa) or wheat flour.

An Interesting Beginning

Excerpt from an article by W. L. Redus
October 17, 1937

In the early 1890s, Mrs. Charles Scheuber and Mrs. Ida L. Turner climbed into a "piano box" buggy and set out to obtain public subscriptions toward the creation of a library. Their efforts received help from an unexpected source—a novel by Daphne du Maurier. "Trilby," swept the country and fanned the spark of the movement to establish a public library in Fort Worth.

(continued on page 25)

Roasted Garlic

Garlic has long been credited for promoting strength and preventing illness. Garlic is easy to grow in the garden and this is a tasty way to benefit from garlic's nutrition.

Garlic bulbs
1 tablespoon olive oil
Chopped fresh or dried herbs

Soak the top of a terra cotta garlic roaster in cold water for 15 minutes. Cut $1/2$ to $3/4$ inch off the tops of garlic bulbs. Remove some but not all of the loose outer skins. Arrange the garlic on the roaster bottom. Drizzle with the olive oil and sprinkle with the herbs. Cover with the top.

Place the garlic roaster in a cold oven. Bake at 325 to 350 degrees for 50 to 60 minutes. Serve the garlic whole. Squeeze each clove and spread on assorted party breads and/or crackers.

If time is of the essence, prepare the garlic as stated and soak the dome. Microwave for 5 to 6 minutes on Medium, or 2 to 4 minutes on High. Test the garlic and microwave for up to 50 seconds longer if needed.

Serves 4 to 6
Marion Edwards, Riverside Branch

Artichoke Squares

1 (6-ounce) jar marinated artichoke hearts
3 or 4 green onions, finely chopped
8 ounces Cheddar cheese, shredded
7 or 8 saltine crackers, crushed
1/8 teaspoon Tabasco sauce
Garlic powder to taste
Pepper to taste
Chopped fresh parsley to taste

Drain the artichokes, reserving the marinade. Sauté the green onions in the reserved marinade in a skillet. Chop the artichokes. Combine the green onions, artichokes, cheese, cracker crumbs, Tabasco sauce, garlic powder, pepper and parsley in a bowl and mix well.

Spoon the artichoke mixture into a baking dish. Bake at 350 degrees for 35 to 40 minutes or until brown and bubbly. Let stand until cool. Cut into squares.

Serves 4 to 6
Sylvia Autrey, Wedgwood Branch

Texas Brownies

1 small can sliced jalapeño chiles
12 ounces Cheddar cheese, shredded
8 eggs

Arrange the jalapeño chiles over the bottom of a 9×13-inch or 8×8-inch baking dish. Sprinkle with the cheese. Beat the eggs in a mixing bowl until blended. Pour over the top.

Bake at 350 degrees for 25 to 30 minutes or until set and light brown. Cool slightly. Cut into squares. Reheat in microwave if desired. Increase the amount of jalapeño chiles for a spicier appetizer.

Serves 12 to 15
Clark Strickland, Ella Mae Shamblee Branch

Armadillo Eggs

15 medium fresh jalapeño chiles
8 ounces Monterey Jack cheese
1½ cups baking mix
8 ounces hot sausage, crumbled
1 egg, beaten
1 (7-ounce) package pork Shake'n Bake
Ranch salad dressing

Make a horizontal slit in the top of each jalapeño chile to form a pocket; discard the seeds. Cut 15 thin slices of cheese and place 1 slice in each pocket. Shred the remaining cheese.

Combine the shredded cheese, baking mix and sausage in a bowl and mix well. Shape some of the sausage mixture around each jalapeño chile to enclose. Dip in the egg and coat with the Shake'n Bake. Arrange the jalapeño chiles in a single layer in a baking pan. Bake at 350 degrees for 20 to 25 minutes or until light brown. Serve with ranch salad dressing.

Serves 15
Missy Strickland, daughter of Clark Strickland, Ella Mae Shamblee Branch

Aunt Ollie's Eggplant Fritters

People in Louisiana love to cook and drink strong coffee. My Aunt Ollie would often make these fritters to go with coffee.

1 eggplant, boiled
3 tablespoons sugar, or 3 envelopes artificial sweetener
2 tablespoons flour
1 egg, beaten
2 cups baking mix

Mash the eggplant, sugar, flour and egg in a bowl until blended. Add the baking mix and stir until the mixture adheres. Drop by teaspoonfuls into hot oil in a skillet. Fry until golden brown; drain. Sprinkle with additional sugar if desired.

Serves 8 to 10
Lynn Allen, Diamond Hill/Jarvis Branch

Jalapeño Squares

1 cup evaporated milk
2 eggs
½ to 1 cup chopped jalapeño chiles
16 ounces Cheddar cheese, shredded
16 ounces Monterey Jack cheese, shredded
1 cup flour

Whisk the evaporated milk and eggs in a bowl until blended. Stir in the jalapeño chiles. Combine the Cheddar cheese, Monterey Jack cheese and flour in a bowl and mix well. Stir the evaporated milk mixture into the cheese mixture.

Spread the cheese mixture in a 9×13-inch baking dish sprayed with nonstick cooking spray. Bake at 350 degrees for 30 minutes. Cool slightly. Cut into squares. Serve warm.

Makes 30 squares
Frances Allen, Ella Mae Shamblee Branch

Poor Man's Rat Toes

12 to 16 Anaheim chiles
1 (10-ounce) can nacho cheese soup

Make a horizontal slit in the top of each Anaheim chile to form a pocket; discard the seeds. Arrange the Anaheim chiles in a single layer in a baking dish. Fill each pocket with some of the soup. Bake at 350 degrees for 15 minutes.

Serves 12 to 16
Lesley Smith, Haltom City Public Library

Paul's Nachos

Tortilla chips
Shredded Cheddar cheese
Refried beans
Sliced black olives

Spread tortilla chips in a single layer on a baking sheet. Sprinkle with cheese. Top with refried beans and sprinkle with olives. Bake at 350 degrees for 15 to 20 minutes or until bubbly. Top with sour cream and hot sauce. Serve with a tossed salad.

Makes a variable amount
Gerry Humphreys, Wedgwood Branch

Roasted Pecans

This recipe is the first recipe in the Library's second cookbook, 641.5, Too. I make these pecans for Christmas gifts every year and I frequently have requests for the recipe.

1 egg white
2 tablespoons water
1/2 cup sugar
1 teaspoon cinnamon
1/2 teaspoon salt
1/4 teaspoon ground cloves
1/4 teaspoon allspice
1 pound pecan halves

Whisk the egg and water in a bowl. Stir in the sugar, cinnamon, salt, cloves and allspice. Add the pecans and stir until coated. Spread the pecans in a single layer on a baking sheet. Bake at 250 degrees for 1 hour. Spread the pecans in a single layer on a sheet of waxed paper. Let stand until cool. Store in an airtight container.

Makes 3 to 4 cups
Lynn Frazier, Southwest Regional Library

Toasted Pecans

These pecans are a favorite at parties and family gatherings. I was given this recipe by a woman from Bells, Texas.

4 cups pecans
¼ cup (½ stick) butter
10 dashes of Tabasco sauce
2 tablespoons garlic salt
1 tablespoon Worcestershire sauce

Spread the pecans in a single layer on a baking sheet. Heat the butter in a saucepan until melted. Stir in the Tabasco sauce, garlic salt and Worcestershire sauce. Drizzle the butter mixture over the pecans and stir until coated. Bake at 300 degrees for 40 to 45 minutes, stirring every 10 minutes.

Makes 4 cups
Betty Wilson, Richland Hills Public Library

Crunchy Pumpkin Seeds

My memories of Halloween involve pumpkin seeds as much as costumes and trick-or-treating. My mother used a different recipe that involved soaking the seeds in brine water for what seemed like an eternity. My sisters and I could hardly wait to eat those seeds, once they finally got roasted. This recipe is much simpler and offers almost instant gratification to the young pumpkin seed eater in my home. My daughter loves to take these roasted seeds to school to introduce her friends to this delicacy.

1 cup unshelled pumpkin seeds
1 tablespoon vegetable oil
½ teaspoon seasoned salt

Rinse the pumpkin seeds. Spread on paper towels to dry. Spread the seeds in a single layer on a baking sheet. Drizzle with the oil. Sprinkle with the seasoned salt. Roast at 225 degrees for 1 hour or until golden brown and crisp, stirring every 15 minutes.

Makes 1 cup
Roberta Schenewerk, Central Library

Honey-Cardamom Crunch

6 cups bite-size rice square cereal
2 cups small pretzel twists
1 cup unblanched whole almonds
1 cup shredded coconut
⅓ cup packed brown sugar
¼ cup (½ stick) butter

¼ cup honey
½ to 1 teaspoon cardamom, or
   ¼ teaspoon allspice
1 cup dried cranberries or chopped
   dried pineapple

Combine the cereal, pretzels, almonds and coconut in a roasting pan and mix well. Combine the brown sugar, butter, honey and cardamom in a saucepan. Cook until blended, stirring frequently. Drizzle the butter mixture over the cereal mixture and toss to coat.

    Bake at 300 degrees for 40 minutes, stirring every 10 minutes. Stir in the cranberries. Spread the cereal mixture on a sheet of foil. Let stand until cool. Store in an airtight container.

Makes 10 cups
Hilda Olson, Central Library

Honey-Roasted Chex Mix

3 cups Honey Nut Chex cereal
2 cups Cheerios cereal
1½ cups Bugles original flavor snacks
1 cup pretzels, or ½ cup honey-
   roasted peanuts

2 tablespoons light corn syrup
2 tablespoons honey
1 tablespoon butter or margarine
½ teaspoon vanilla extract

Combine the cereals, snacks and pretzels in a bowl and toss to mix. Combine the corn syrup, honey and butter in a saucepan. Bring to a boil over medium heat, stirring occasionally. Remove from heat. Stir in the vanilla. Pour the corn syrup mixture over the cereal mixture and toss to coat.

    Spread the cereal mixture in an ungreased 9×13-inch baking pan. Bake at 325 degrees for 12 minutes; stir. Bake for 12 minutes longer. Spread on waxed paper or foil. Let stand until cool. Break into bite-size pieces. Store in an airtight container. May bake in an ungreased 10×15-inch baking sheet with sides for 20 minutes, stirring halfway through the baking process.

Makes 7 cups
Karen Brown, Central Library

SOUPS & SANDWICHES

sand·wich (sănd′wĭch) *n.*

Two or more slices of bread with a layer of
meat, cheese, etc., between them.

Shown above: The reading room from the Carnegie Public Library, 1901-1938

Black Bean Soup

2 cups dried black beans
3 ounces smoked slab bacon, finely chopped
1 large onion, chopped
2 jalapeño or serrano chiles, minced
1 tablespoon cumin
1 teaspoon ground coriander
1 (16-ounce) can diced tomatoes
4 to 5 cups chicken broth
1 cup sour cream
Salt to taste
Cayenne pepper to taste

Sort and rinse the beans. Combine the beans with a generous amount of water in a bowl. Let stand for 8 to 10 hours; drain.

Cook the bacon in an uncovered pressure cooker over medium heat for 3 minutes or until the fat is rendered. Add the onion and jalapeño chiles. Cook for 7 to 9 minutes or until the onion is tender, stirring occasionally. Stir in the cumin and coriander. Cook for 1 minute. Add the beans, undrained tomatoes and 4 cups of the broth.

Cover the pressure cooker. Bring to high pressure. Reduce the heat to stabilize the pressure. Cook for 15 minutes. Release the pressure naturally. Transfer 2 to 3 cups of the bean mixture to a blender or food processor container. Process until puréed. Stir the purée into the soup mixture. Add the sour cream, salt and cayenne pepper and mix well. Add the remaining 1 cup broth if desired for a thinner consistency and mix well. Cook just until heated through, stirring frequently. Ladle into soup bowls.

Serves 6 to 8
Renée Cordray, Ridglea Branch

Pressure cooker
A cooking pot with a locking, airtight lid and valve system to regulate pressure; food is quickly cooked under the high heat of steam pressure.

Christmas Eve Crab Chowder

Served with a salad and crusty bread, this light meal is the perfect prelude to the feasting that would follow on Christmas Day.

3 tablespoons butter
2 ribs celery, chopped
3 cups water
2 potatoes, peeled, chopped
1/4 cup minced onion
6 ounces crab meat, shells removed
1 quart milk
1 cup shredded Cheddar cheese
1 1/4 teaspoons salt
1/4 teaspoon ground white pepper

Heat the butter in a large saucepan until melted. Stir in the celery. Cook until tender-crisp, stirring frequently. Add the water, potatoes and onion and mix well. Cook for 15 minutes or until the potatoes are tender, stirring occasionally. Add the crab meat and mix well. Stir in the milk, cheese, salt and white pepper.

Cook over low heat until the cheese melts and the soup is heated through, stirring occasionally. Ladle into soup bowls.

Serves 8
Roberta Schenewerk, Central Library

Assistance from Andrew Carnegie

Efforts to raise funds for the library were hindered by the panic of 1893. An enterprising supporter thought of asking the aid of Andrew Carnegie, the philanthropist who gave millions toward the establishment of libraries. A neatly worded request by Mrs. D. B. Keeler evoked a response. Mrs. Keeler asked the philanthropist for a contribution of "the price of a cigar." In a letter from Skibo Castle, Scotland, Carnegie replied that he would do a little better—with certain provisions. He offered to donate $50,000 for the erection of a building, provided the library association would equip it and furnish not less than $10,000 worth of books, and that the city would pledge $4,000 annually for its upkeep.

Lentil and Portobello Soup

My husband is on a reduced-fat diet so we partake of many vegetarian dishes. This soup pleases carnivores as well as vegetarians.

1 cup dried brown lentils
1 onion, chopped
3 garlic cloves, minced
2 teaspoons olive oil
1 pound portobello mushrooms,
   chopped

4 cups vegetable or chicken broth
1 (14-ounce) can diced Italian-style
   tomatoes
Salt and black pepper to taste
Garlic pepper to taste
1/2 cup chopped fresh parsley

Sort and rinse the lentils. Sauté the onion and garlic in the olive oil in a saucepan until the onion is tender. Stir in the mushrooms. Cook until the mushrooms are tender and have released their liquid, stirring occasionally. Add the lentils and broth and mix well. Bring to a boil; reduce heat. Simmer for 30 minutes, stirring occasionally. Add the undrained tomatoes, salt, black pepper and garlic pepper and mix well. Simmer for 30 minutes longer, stirring occasionally. Ladle into soup bowls. Sprinkle with the parsley.

Serves 4 to 6
Lynn Frazier, Southwest Regional Library

Creamy Swiss Onion Soup

This is a creamy variation of the classic French onion soup.

2 large onions, sliced
1/4 cup (1/2 stick) butter
1/4 cup flour
3 cups chicken broth
3 cups milk

4 cups shredded Swiss cheese
6 slices French bread, toasted
1 cup shredded Swiss cheese
   (optional)

Sauté the onions in the butter in a saucepan for 10 minutes. Stir in the flour. Cook until bubbly, stirring constantly. Add the broth and mix well. Cook until slightly thickened, stirring occasionally. Stir in the milk. Bring just to a boil, stirring constantly. Stir in 4 cups cheese. Cook just until the cheese melts, stirring constantly. Remove from heat. Place 1 slice of toasted French bread in each of 6 soup bowls. Ladle the soup over the bread. Sprinkle with 1 cup cheese. Serve immediately.

Serves 6
Roberta Schenewerk, Central Library

Italian Sausage Soup

1 pound Italian sausage, coarsely chopped
5 ounces meat tortellini or cheese tortellini
5 cups beef broth
2 cups canned stewed no-added-salt tomatoes
1½ cups sliced unpeeled zucchini
1 cup thinly sliced carrots, parboiled
1 (8-ounce) can tomato sauce
1 cup chopped onion
½ cup water
½ cup dry red wine
2 garlic cloves, minced
½ teaspoon basil
½ teaspoon oregano
½ teaspoon parsley flakes

Brown the sausage in a stockpot; drain. Add the tortellini, broth, tomatoes, zucchini, carrots, tomato sauce, onion, water, wine, garlic, basil, oregano and parsley flakes and mix well. Bring to a boil; reduce heat.

Simmer for 1 hour, stirring occasionally. Ladle into soup bowls. Serve with crusty bread. The flavor of the soup is enhanced if prepared 1 day in advance and stored, covered, in the refrigerator. Reheat just before serving.

Serves 6
Connie Sullivan, Keller Public Library

Zucchini (zoo·KEE·nee)
A cylindrical summer squash with smooth, green skin and a light delicate flavor.

Taco Soup

2 pounds ground beef
1 large onion, chopped
2 (14-ounce) cans stewed tomatoes
1 (16-ounce) can ranch-style beans
1 (16-ounce) can corn, drained
1 (16-ounce) can hominy, drained
1 (15-ounce) can lima beans, drained
1 (15-ounce) can pinto beans, drained
1½ cups beef broth
1 envelope ranch salad dressing mix
1 envelope taco seasoning mix
Salt and pepper to taste
Tortilla chips
Shredded Cheddar cheese

Brown the ground beef with the onion in a stockpot, stirring until the ground beef is crumbly; drain. Stir in the undrained tomatoes, undrained ranch-style beans, corn, hominy, lima beans, pinto beans, broth, dressing mix, seasoning mix, salt and pepper.

Cook just until heated through, stirring frequently. Ladle into soup bowls. Serve with tortilla chips and shredded cheese.

Serves 10
Roberta Schenewerk, Central Library

Hominy (HA·mah·nee)
Corn kernels, dried by soaking in lime or lye; reconstituted before canning.

Secret Ingredient Chili

This recipe is a staff chili cook-off winner.

1 pound ground hot pork sausage
3 pounds beef sirloin,
    cut into 1/2-inch cubes
1 tablespoon vegetable oil
1 (14-ounce) can beef broth
1 (8-ounce) can tomato sauce
1 (6-ounce) can spicy tomato juice
3/4 cup beer
1/2 cup chopped sun-dried tomatoes
3 tablespoons chili powder, or to taste
1 tablespoon sugar

1 tablespoon onion powder
2 teaspoons red hot pepper sauce
1 teaspoon garlic powder
1/2 teaspoon salt
1/2 teaspoon cumin
1/2 teaspoon Worcestershire sauce
1/4 teaspoon allspice
Hot cooked rice
Shredded cheese
Chopped onions
Sour cream

Brown the sausage in a stockpot, stirring until crumbly. Drain in a colander. Brown the beef in the oil in the stockpot, turning frequently. Return the sausage to the stockpot. Add the broth, tomato sauce, tomato juice, beer, sun-dried tomatoes, chili powder, sugar, onion powder, hot pepper sauce, garlic powder, salt, cumin, Worcestershire sauce and allspice and mix well. Bring to a boil; reduce heat.

Simmer, covered, for 1 1/2 hours or until the beef is tender, stirring occasionally; remove cover. Cook for 30 minutes longer or until of the desired consistency, stirring occasionally. Spoon the chili over hot cooked rice in chili bowls. Garnish with cheese, onions and sour cream. Spoon the chili over corn chips or a baked potato for variety.

Serves 12
Roberta Schenewerk, Central Library

Vegetarian Chili

2 onions, chopped
1 green bell pepper, chopped
2 ribs celery, chopped
6 garlic cloves, minced
1 to 2 tablespoons olive oil
1 tablespoon chili powder
2 teaspoons basil
2 teaspoons oregano
1 teaspoon cumin
½ teaspoon cayenne pepper
Hot pepper sauce to taste
1 (16-ounce) can hominy, drained, rinsed
5 (15-ounce) cans beans, such as kidney beans, black beans and/or
   great Northern beans, drained, rinsed
1 (26-ounce) jar reduced-fat spaghetti sauce
1 (15-ounce) can diced tomatoes
1 (15-ounce) can tomatoes with chiles
1 potato, chopped
1 to 2 cups water

Sauté the onions, bell pepper, celery and garlic in the olive oil in a stockpot for 5 minutes or until the onion is tender. Stir in the chili powder, basil, oregano, cumin, cayenne pepper and hot pepper sauce. Cook for 3 minutes, stirring occasionally. Add the hominy and beans and mix well. Stir in the spaghetti sauce, undrained tomatoes, potato and 1 cup of the water. Bring to a boil; reduce heat.

Simmer for 45 minutes, stirring occasionally and adding the remaining 1 cup water as needed for the desired consistency. Taste and adjust seasonings. Ladle into chili bowls.

For those meat lovers, you may add 1 pound browned ground beef or turkey. Additional water and another jar of spaghetti sauce will probably be required.

Serves 10 to 12
Lynn Frazier, Southwest Regional Library

Chili

This chili recipe was the prize winner at the 2000 Christmas party.

1 pound ground beef
1 large onion, chopped
1/4 teaspoon salt
2 (16-ounce) cans diced tomatoes
2 (16-ounce) cans kidney beans,
    drained

1 (16-ounce) jar spaghetti sauce
1/2 cup ketchup
1/2 teaspoon chili powder
1/2 teaspoon garlic salt
1/4 teaspoon sugar

Brown the ground beef with the onion and salt in a stockpot, stirring until the ground beef is crumbly; drain. Stir in the undrained tomatoes, beans, spaghetti sauce, ketchup, chili powder, garlic salt and sugar. Bring to a boil; reduce heat. Simmer for 1 hour, stirring occasionally. Taste and adjust the seasonings. Ladle into chili bowls.

Serves 4 to 6
Melva Siddiq, Floater

Brunswick Stew

2 (3-pound) chickens, cut into pieces
1 to 2 quarts water
2 (16-ounce) cans tomatoes
2 (16-ounce) cans corn
2 large onions, sliced
2 cups lima beans

2 cups cut okra (optional)
3 medium potatoes, chopped
1 tablespoon salt
1 tablespoon sugar
1 teaspoon pepper

For a thick stew, combine the chickens with 1 quart of the water in a stockpot; add more water for a thinner consistency. Bring to a boil; reduce heat. Simmer for 2 1/4 hours or until the chicken can be easily removed from the bones. Remove the chicken to a bowl with a slotted spoon, reserving the broth. Add the undrained tomatoes, undrained corn, onions, lima beans, okra and potatoes and mix well.

Cook until the potatoes are tender, stirring occasionally. Chop the chicken, discarding the skin and bones. Return the chicken to the stockpot. Stir in the salt, sugar and pepper. Cook just until heated through, stirring occasionally. Ladle into individual bowls. Tastes even better the next day.

Serves 8 to 10
Frances Allen, Ella Mae Shamblee Branch

Fortunately, the site for the library building was not a problem. In 1892, Mrs. Sarah G. Jennings had given permission for a library to be erected on part of a tract known as Hyde Park. Her consent provided that the land might not only be used for library purposes, but for "such mental and moral training and improvement" as seemed fit and proper to the library association.

Italian Beef Sandwiches

Excellent served on Christmas Eve, New Year's Eve, and for summer parties.

1 (4-pound) boneless beef sirloin or rolled rump roast, trimmed
$\frac{1}{2}$ cup water
1 envelope Italian salad dressing mix
2 teaspoons crushed Italian seasoning
$\frac{1}{2}$ to 1 teaspoon crushed red pepper
$\frac{1}{2}$ teaspoon garlic powder
10 to 12 Kaiser rolls or sandwich rolls, split
Roasted red pepper strips (optional)

Cut the beef into 2- to 3-inch pieces. Place in a slow cooker. Combine the water, dressing mix, Italian seasoning, red pepper and garlic powder in a bowl and mix well. Pour over the beef in the slow cooker and stir to coat.

Cook, covered, on Low for 10 to 12 hours, or on High for 5 to 6 hours. Remove the beef with a slotted spoon to a cutting board. Shred using 2 forks.

Spoon the shredded beef onto the bottom halves of the rolls. Arrange red pepper strips over the beef and drizzle with some of the pan juices if desired. Top with the roll tops. May substitute 1 loaf of French bread, split into halves, for the rolls.

Makes 10 to 12 sandwiches
Hilda Olson, Central Library

The Ultimate Grilled Cheese

3/4 cup mayonnaise
3 ounces cream cheese, softened
1 cup shredded Cheddar cheese
1 cup shredded mozzarella cheese
1/2 teaspoon garlic powder
1/8 teaspoon seasoned salt
10 (1/2-inch-thick) slices Italian bread
2 tablespoons margarine, softened

Beat the mayonnaise and cream cheese in a mixing bowl until smooth. Stir in the Cheddar cheese, mozzarella cheese, garlic powder and seasoned salt. Spread 1 side of 5 slices of the bread with approximately 1/3 cup of the cheese mixture. Top with the remaining bread slices.

Spread the margarine on both sides of the sandwiches. Cook in a skillet over medium heat until golden brown on both sides, turning once. Serve immediately.

Makes 5 sandwiches
Sylvia Autrey, Wedgwood Branch

Mozzarella (maht·suh·REHL·lah)
A mild, white, fresh cheese originally made from the milk of water buffalos.

Crowd-Pleasing Heroes

This is a very versatile recipe and all that is required is your imagination. Substitute dark breads for the light breads, add a little mustard or horseradish to the spread for a slightly different flavor or substitute different meats for the ones mentioned. Be creative!

2 unsliced loaves Italian or sourdough bread
8 ounces cream cheese, softened
1/4 cup mayonnaise
3/4 cup chopped red onion
1 tablespoon Worcestershire sauce
1 pound cooked ham, thinly sliced
1 pound roast beef, thinly sliced
14 dill pickle slices

Cut the loaves horizontally into halves. Remove the centers, leaving 1/2-inch shells. Reserve the centers for another use. Beat the cream cheese and mayonnaise in a mixing bowl until blended. Stir in the onion and Worcestershire sauce.

Spread the cream cheese mixture over the cut sides of the bread halves. Layer the ham and beef over the cream cheese mixture. Arrange the pickle slices on the bottom halves of the loaves. Press the halves together gently. Wrap each loaf separately in plastic wrap. Chill for 2 hours or longer. Cut into 1 1/2-inch slices.

Serves 14
Roberta Schenewerk, Central Library

SALADS

sal·ad (săl′əd) *n.*

Any of various cold dishes, consisting of
vegetables, fruit or meat, served with dressing.

Shown above: Carnegie Public Library, Demolition, 1938

Bing Cherry Salad

1 (16-ounce) can Bing cherries
1 (3-ounce) package cherry gelatin
Juice of 1 orange
Juice of 1 lemon

Drain the cherries, reserving the juice. Pit the cherries. Heat the reserved juice in a saucepan. Add the gelatin, stirring until dissolved.

Combine the orange juice and lemon juice in a measuring cup. Add enough water to measure 1 cup. Add the juice mixture to the gelatin mixture and mix well. Stir in the cherries. Pour into a shallow dish. Chill until set.

Serves 6
Raydene Rankin, Southwest Regional Library

Cherry Gelatin with Sherry

1 (15-ounce) can black or Royal Anne cherries, or to taste
1 (3-ounce) package black or red cherry gelatin
½ cup boiling water
½ cup sherry
Chopped pecans

Drain the cherries, reserving 1 cup of the juice. Dissolve the gelatin in the boiling water in a heatproof bowl and mix well. Stir in the reserved juice. Chill until partially set. Stir in the cherries, sherry and pecans. Pour into a shallow dish. Chill until set. If using frozen or fresh cherries substitute 1 cup water for the cherry juice.

Serves 6
Sarah Harris, Riverside Branch

Mom's Cranberry Salad

1 package fresh cranberries, rinsed
1 (6-ounce) package strawberry-banana gelatin
2 cups boiling water
2 cups water
2 cups sugar
1 (15-ounce) can fruit cocktail
1 (3-ounce) can shredded coconut
2 ounces pecan pieces

Combine the cranberries with enough water to cover in a saucepan. Bring to a boil. Boil until the cranberries pop; drain.

Dissolve the gelatin in 2 cups boiling water in a heatproof bowl and mix well. Stir in the cranberries, 2 cups water, sugar, fruit cocktail, coconut and pecans. Pour into a dish or mold. Chill until set.

Serves 6
Martha Carter, Central Library

Frozen Cranberry Banana Salad

1 (20-ounce) can juice-pack pineapple tidbits
5 firm medium bananas, cut lengthwise into halves, sliced
1 (16-ounce) can whole cranberry sauce
½ cup sugar
12 ounces whipped topping
½ cup chopped pecans

Drain the pineapple, reserving the juice. Combine the reserved juice and bananas in a bowl and toss to coat. Combine the cranberry sauce and sugar in a bowl and mix well. Drain the bananas and stir the bananas into the cranberry mixture. Add the pineapple, whipped topping and pecans and stir to combine.

Spoon the cranberry mixture into a 9×12-inch dish. Freeze until firm. Let stand at room temperature for 15 minutes before serving.

Serves 12 to 16
Mary Taggart Sikes, Central Library

Under the Sea Salad

3/4 cup pineapple juice
24 large marshmallows, chopped, or 240 miniature marshmallows
1 cup chopped pecans
3 ounces cream cheese, softened
1 cup whipped cream
1 (3-ounce) package lime gelatin

Heat the pineapple juice in a saucepan just until the juice begins to boil. Remove from heat. Add the marshmallows and stir until the marshmallows melt. Combine the pecans and cream cheese in a bowl and mix until the pecans are coated. Add the cream cheese to the juice mixture and mix well. Let stand until cool. Fold in the whipped cream. Spoon into a shallow dish. Chill until firm.

Prepare the gelatin using package directions. Let stand until thickened. Pour gently over the prepared layer. Chill until set.

Serves 12
Raydene Rankin, Southwest Regional Library

Winter Fruit Salad

2 cups pineapple chunks
2 bananas, sliced
1 cup seedless green grapes
1 cup pitted dates
1 cup sliced oranges
Salad greens

Toss the pineapple, bananas, grapes, dates and oranges in a bowl. Spoon the fruit salad over the salad greens on salad plates. Serve immediately.

Serves 4 to 6
Karen Brown, Central Library

Fresh Broccoli Salad

SALAD
Florets of 1 large bunch broccoli
1 small red onion, chopped
1 cup raisins
1/2 cup bacon bits
1/2 cup sunflower seed kernels

DRESSING
1 cup mayonnaise
1/4 cup sugar
2 tablespoons vinegar

For the salad, toss the broccoli, onion, raisins, bacon bits and sunflower seed kernels in a salad bowl.

For the dressing, combine the mayonnaise, sugar and vinegar in a bowl and mix well. Add the dressing to the broccoli mixture and mix until coated. Store, covered, in the refrigerator until serving time.

Serves 8
Rina Lutts, Haltom City Public Library

Scandinavian Cucumbers

1/2 cup sour cream
2 tablespoons snipped fresh parsley
2 tablespoons tarragon vinegar
1 tablespoon finely chopped onion
1 tablespoon sugar
1/4 teaspoon dillweed
3 small unpeeled cucumbers, thinly
  sliced (about 3 cups)

Combine the sour cream, parsley, tarragon vinegar, onion, sugar and dillweed in a bowl and mix well. Fold in the cucumbers. Chill, covered, for 2 hours.

Serves 6
Frances Allen, Ella Mae Shamblee Branch

Tarragon (TEHR·uh·gon)
An aromatic herb, native to Siberia, known for its anise-like flavor. Widely used in classic French cooking.

Fry's Famous Italian Salad

I guarantee all other salads will pale in comparison! Decrease the recipe by half for smaller crowds.

ITALIAN VINAIGRETTE
2 cups vegetable oil
1 cup white wine vinegar
6 anchovies
1/4 cup cornstarch
3 tablespoons sugar
1 tablespoon salt
3/4 teaspoon oregano
1/2 teaspoon pepper
1/2 teaspoon garlic salt

SALAD
1 head iceberg lettuce, torn into bite-size pieces
1 head romaine, torn into bite-size pieces
1 small red bell pepper, chopped
Chopped green onion tops to taste
Shredded provolone cheese to taste
Shredded mozzarella cheese to taste
Grated Romano cheese to taste
Grated Parmesan cheese to taste
Croutons

For the vinaigrette, combine the oil, wine vinegar, anchovies, cornstarch, sugar, salt, oregano, pepper and garlic salt in a blender container. Process until smooth.

   For the salad, toss the iceberg lettuce, romaine, bell pepper, green onion tops, provolone cheese, mozzarella cheese, Romano cheese and Parmesan cheese in a large salad bowl. Pour the vinaigrette over the top. Marinate at room temperature for 1 to 2 hours. Sprinkle with croutons before serving.

Serves 10 to 12
Eric Fry, Central Library

Green and White Layered Spinach Salad

PARMESAN DRESSING
2 cups mayonnaise
¾ cup grated Parmesan cheese
¼ cup milk
1 tablespoon dried chives
2 teaspoons white vinegar
1 teaspoon garlic powder
½ teaspoon Worcestershire sauce

SALAD
2 packages fresh baby spinach, trimmed
1 cup shredded Swiss cheese
6 hard-cooked eggs, sliced
½ medium red onion, chopped
1 pound bacon, crisp-cooked, drained, crumbled
2 cups sliced fresh mushrooms
1 pint cherry tomatoes

For the dressing, combine the mayonnaise, cheese, milk, chives, vinegar, garlic powder and Worcestershire sauce in a bowl and mix well.

For the salad, layer the spinach, cheese, eggs, onion, bacon and mushrooms in a large flat-bottom bowl in the order listed. Spread the dressing over the top, sealing to the edge. Top with the cherry tomatoes. Chill until serving time.

Serves 8
Roberta Schenewerk, Central Library

The Building Begins

The cornerstone was laid in 1900 with appropriate ceremonies by the Masonic Grand Lodge. And, in October of 1901, the Carnegie Public Library in Fort Worth, Texas, officially opened its doors with Mrs. Charles Scheuber as Librarian and 6,907 volumes on the shelves. The Library included a Depository for Government Documents and the Fort Worth Museum of Art.

Basil Cherry Tomatoes

3 pints cherry tomatoes, cut into halves
1/2 cup chopped fresh basil
1 1/2 teaspoons olive or vegetable oil
Salt and pepper to taste
Lettuce leaves (optional)

Combine the cherry tomatoes, basil, olive oil, salt and pepper in a bowl and mix gently. Chill, covered, until serving time. Spoon the cherry tomato salad onto lettuce-lined salad plates.

Serves 4 to 6
Sylvia Autrey, Wedgwood Branch

Marinated Vegetable Salad

3/4 cup cider vinegar
1/2 cup salad oil
2 tablespoons sugar
1 teaspoon salt
1/4 teaspoon pepper
2 (16-ounce) cans French-style green beans, drained
1 (16-ounce) can whole kernel corn, drained
Florets of 1/2 small head cauliflower, cut into bite-size pieces
1/2 medium red onion, thinly sliced, separated into rings

Whisk the vinegar, salad oil, sugar, salt and pepper in a bowl. Add the green beans, corn, cauliflower and onion and toss to coat. Chill, covered, for 4 hours or longer, stirring occasionally. May store, covered, for up to 3 to 4 days in the refrigerator. The onion flavor will intensify with age.

Serves 6 to 8
Frances Allen, Ella Mae Shamblee Branch

Southwestern Barbecue Pasta Salad

When I was in college one of the favorite places to go for a special occasion was the Clay Pot Eatery in Krum, Texas. The restaurant has closed, but this recipe is an attempt to capture the flavor of my favorite pasta salad from their humongous salad bar. I now make this salad every Fourth of July.

16 ounces mostaccioli or radiatore
8 ounces barbecue beef, chopped
8 ounces sharp Cheddar cheese, cut into strips
1 (6-ounce) can pitted black olives, drained, cut into halves
4 ounces oil-pack sun-dried tomatoes, julienned
1 cup barbecue sauce
1 bell pepper, roasted, peeled, julienned
½ cup chopped red onion

Cook the pasta using package directions. Rinse with cold water and drain. Toss the pasta, barbecue beef, cheese, olives, sun-dried tomatoes, barbecue sauce, roasted pepper and onion in a bowl. Chill, covered, for several hours to allow the flavors to meld. The flavor is enhanced if the salad is brought to room temperature before serving. For a fun touch, use other pastas. For example, those that are shaped like stars or the state of Texas.

Serves 6
Roberta Schenewerk, Central Library

Mostaccioli (mos·tah·chee·OH·lee)
Two-inch-long pasta tubes cut on the diagonal.

Radiatore (rah·dyah·TOH·ray)
One-inch-long pasta tubes with rippled edges.

Mexican Salad

2 tomatoes, chopped
1 (15-ounce) can ranch-style beans, drained, rinsed
1 small onion, chopped (optional)
1 head lettuce, torn into bite-size pieces

10 ounces mild longhorn cheese, shredded
1 bottle Catalina salad dressing
1 (7-ounce) package corn chips

Layer the tomatoes, beans, onion and lettuce in a salad bowl in the order listed. Chill, covered, in the refrigerator. Add the cheese, 3/4 bottle of the salad dressing and the corn chips to the chilled lettuce mixture and toss to mix.

Serves 6
Sylvia Autrey, Wedgwood Branch

Mom's Taco Salad

So good, it has to be Mom's!

SOUTH SEAS DRESSING
1 cup vegetable oil
1 cup sugar
1 cup ketchup
3/4 cup vinegar
2 teaspoons salt
1 garlic clove, minced
Grated onion to taste

SALAD
8 ounces ground beef
1 envelope taco seasoning mix
1 head lettuce, torn into bite-size pieces
2 tomatoes, chopped
1 cup shredded Cheddar cheese
1 onion, chopped
Doritos or taco chips, crumbled
1 (8-ounce) can kidney beans, drained

For the dressing, combine the oil, sugar, ketchup, vinegar, salt, garlic and onion in a jar with a tight-fitting lid. Seal tightly and shake to mix. Chill until serving time. May be processed in a blender or food processor.

For the salad, brown the ground beef in a skillet, stirring until crumbly; drain. Stir in the taco seasoning mix. Toss the ground beef mixture, lettuce, tomatoes, cheese, onion, chips and kidney beans in a salad bowl. Add about 1/4 cup, or the desired amount, of the dressing to the salad and toss to coat. Serve immediately. May substitute Catalina salad dressing for the South Seas Dressing.

Serves 4 to 6
Eric Fry, Central Library

Simple Chicken Salad

Serve on raisin bread for a real treat.

4 cups chopped cooked chicken
1 cup chopped celery
½ cup chopped onion

1 cup mayonnaise-type salad dressing
   or mayonnaise
½ cup sour cream

Combine the chicken, celery and onion in a bowl and mix well. Stir in the salad dressing and sour cream. Chill, covered, until serving time. May substitute a mixture of ½ cup salad dressing and ½ cup mayonnaise for the salad dressing or mayonnaise.

Serves 6 to 8
Barbara M. Smith, Central Library (retired)

Chinese Chicken Salad

SALAD
2 chicken breasts, cooked
1 head cabbage, finely chopped
3 or 4 green onions, chopped
3 to 4 ounces slivered almonds,
   toasted
3 tablespoons sesame seeds, toasted
1 (3-ounce) package ramen noodles,
   broken

SEASONED DRESSING
½ cup salad oil
3 tablespoons rice wine vinegar
2 tablespoons sugar
1 ramen noodle flavoring envelope
1 teaspoon salt
Pepper to taste

For the salad, shred the chicken, discarding the skin and bones. Combine the chicken, cabbage, green onions, almonds, sesame seeds and ramen noodles in a salad bowl and mix well.

    For the dressing, whisk the salad oil, wine vinegar, sugar, flavoring envelope, salt and pepper in a bowl. Drizzle over the salad and toss to coat.

Serves 4 to 6
Barb Grisell, Summerglen Branch

Curried Apple and Chicken Salad

SALAD
2 tablespoons lemon juice
1 tablespoon salad oil
2 Granny Smith apples, chopped
3½ cups chopped cooked chicken
1⅓ cups cooked rice

CURRY CASHEW DRESSING
1 cup mayonnaise
½ cup chopped cashews
2 tablespoons chopped fresh parsley
1 tablespoon chopped onion
2 teaspoons curry powder
1 teaspoon salt

For the salad, whisk the lemon juice and salad oil in a salad bowl. Add the apples and toss to coat. Stir in the chopped chicken and cooked rice.

For the dressing, combine the mayonnaise, cashews, parsley, onion, curry powder and salt in a bowl and mix well. Add the dressing to the chicken mixture and mix well. Chill, covered, until serving time. Arrange on salad plates. Garnish with apple wedges and additional parsley.

Serves 6 to 8
Dorothy Douglas, Haltom City Public Library

Layered Chicken Fajita Salad

This is a meal in a salad that can be prepared very simply with convenience foods purchased at your favorite supermarket.

CHICKEN
4 boneless skinless chicken breasts
¼ cup vegetable oil
2 tablespoons lemon juice
1 teaspoon seasoned salt
1 teaspoon oregano
1 teaspoon garlic powder
½ teaspoon chili powder
½ teaspoon cumin

GUACAMOLE
2 ripe avocados
1 tablespoon lemon juice

SALSA RANCH DRESSING
¾ cup buttermilk
¾ cup mayonnaise
¼ cup salsa
1 envelope buttermilk ranch salad
    dressing mix

SALAD AND ASSEMBLY
1 head lettuce, shredded
1 (15-ounce) can black beans, drained,
    rinsed
1 cup shredded sharp Cheddar cheese
½ medium red onion, chopped
Sliced black olives
Sliced jalapeño chiles

For the chicken, place the chicken breasts in a sealable plastic bag. Whisk the oil, lemon juice, seasoned salt, oregano, garlic powder, chili powder and cumin in bowl. Pour the oil mixture over the chicken and seal tightly. Turn to coat. Marinate in the refrigerator for 8 to 10 hours, turning occasionally; drain. Grill the chicken over hot coals until the juices run clear, turning once or twice. Let stand until cool. Cut into thin slices.

For the guacamole, mash the avocados with the lemon juice in a bowl and mix well.

For the dressing, combine the buttermilk, mayonnaise and salsa in a bowl and mix well. Stir in the dressing mix. Chill, covered, for 30 minutes or until thickened.

For the salad, layer the lettuce, beans, cheese, onion, chicken and guacamole in a salad bowl in the order listed. Spread with the dressing, sealing to the edge. Sprinkle with olives and/or jalapeño chiles. Serve with warm flour tortillas or tortilla chips.

Serves 6
Roberta Schenewerk, Central Library

Kentucky Chef's Salad

½ head iceberg lettuce, shredded
3 heads Bibb lettuce, or ½ head
   Boston lettuce, separated
¼ cup (or more) French salad
   dressing
2 hard-cooked eggs, cut into quarters

2 ripe tomatoes, peeled, cut into
   quarters
¾ cup julienned baked chicken
5 slices bacon, crisp-cooked,
   crumbled
¼ cup French salad dressing

Combine the iceberg lettuce and Bibb lettuce in a salad bowl and mix well. Add ¼ cup (or more) salad dressing and toss to coat. Arrange the eggs and tomatoes around the outer edge of the bowl. Mound the chicken in the center of the bowl. Sprinkle the bacon over the chicken. Drizzle with ¼ cup salad dressing.

Serves 6
Sylvia Autrey, Wedgwood Branch

South Seas Chicken Salad

3 cups chopped cooked chicken
1 head lettuce, shredded
1 cup chopped celery
1 red onion, chopped
¼ cup chopped cashews, toasted
2 mangoes, peeled, chopped (optional)

2 tablespoons lemon juice
1 cup plain yogurt or sour cream
2 teaspoons curry powder
1 teaspoon cumin
Salt and pepper to taste

Combine the chicken, lettuce, celery, onion, cashews, mangoes and lemon juice in a bowl and mix well. Combine the yogurt, curry powder, cumin, salt and pepper in a bowl and mix well. Add the yogurt mixture to the chicken mixture and toss to coat. Serve immediately.

Serves 4
Frances Allen, Ella Mae Shamblee Branch

Mango (MANG·goh)
An oval-shaped tropical fruit native to India; when ripe the green skin will have turned mostly red, blushed with yellow and begun to wrinkle.

Tangy Tuna Cocktail

SALAD
1 (9-ounce) can light tuna,
    drained, flaked
½ cup thinly sliced radishes
2 hard-cooked eggs, chopped
¼ cup chopped dill pickles

TANGY DRESSING
1 teaspoon Dijon mustard
1 teaspoon lemon juice
1 teaspoon white wine vinegar
¼ teaspoon salt
⅛ teaspoon cayenne pepper
2 tablespoons salad oil

For the salad, combine the tuna, radishes, eggs and pickles in a bowl and mix gently.

For the dressing, mix the Dijon mustard, lemon juice, wine vinegar, salt and cayenne pepper in a bowl. Add the salad oil gradually, stirring constantly with a fork until blended. Add the dressing to the salad and mix gently. Chill, covered, for 30 minutes.

Spoon the tuna salad onto a platter lined with shredded lettuce. Sprinkle with parsley. Garnish with lemon wedges.

Serves 4
Corina Escamilla, Wedgwood Branch

Creamy Date Dressing

1 cup vanilla yogurt
Juice of 1 orange (½ cup)
1 teaspoon grated orange zest

6 pitted dates
1 teaspoon curry powder (optional)

Combine the vanilla yogurt, orange juice, orange zest, dates and curry powder in a blender container. Process for 30 seconds or until smooth. Serve with a fruit salad made of pineapple, bananas, grapes, oranges and dates.

Makes 1½ cups
Karen Brown, Central Library

Honey Dijon Salad Dressing

2 tablespoons honey
2 tablespoons vinegar
½ cup vegetable oil
¼ cup mayonnaise
2 tablespoons minced onion
2 tablespoons minced fresh parsley
1 tablespoon Dijon mustard

Whisk the honey and vinegar in a bowl until blended. Add the oil, mayonnaise, onion, parsley and Dijon mustard and stir until mixed. Toss 1 head torn lettuce, ½ sliced cucumber, 1 chopped tomato, 1 chopped green onion and 1 drained 11-ounce can mandarin oranges in a bowl and drizzle with the dressing, or serve with your favorite tossed green salad.

Makes ¾ cup
Gena Fisher, Central Library

Penn Alps Salad Dressing

In the 1930s, a group of women in my hometown sent money to a company in Pennsylvania for this recipe.

1½ cups salad oil
1 cup sugar
1 cup ketchup
½ cup vinegar
½ teaspoon grated onion
½ teaspoon celery seeds
½ teaspoon paprika
½ teaspoon salt

Combine the salad oil, sugar, ketchup, vinegar, onion, celery seeds, paprika and salt in a blender container. Process until smooth. Store, covered, in the refrigerator. Serve with your favorite tossed green salad.

Makes 1 quart
Betty Patterson, Richland Hills Public Library

ENTREES
BEEF & PORK FAVORITES

fa·vor·ites (fāʹvər·its) *n.*

Items regarded with particular
preference or approval.

Shown above: Carnegie Public Library, Art Gallery, 1901-1938

Roast Beef

1 (10-ounce) can roasted garlic soup
2 envelopes onion soup mix
3 to 4 soup cans water
1 (3- to 4-pound) beef pot or shoulder roast

Combine the soup and soup mix in a large roasting pan and mix well. Stir in the water. Place the roast in the pan. Bake, covered, at 350 degrees for 4 to 6 hours or until tender, basting occasionally.

Serves 6 to 8
Brenda McCrary, Richland Hills Public Library

Smothered Beef Roast

1 (2½-pound) beef round or chuck roast, 1 inch thick
Salt and pepper to taste
1 (20-ounce) can diced tomatoes
½ cup chopped green bell pepper
¼ cup chopped onion
1 cup water

Place the roast in a roasting pan. Sprinkle with salt and pepper. Pour the undrained tomatoes over the roast. Sprinkle with the bell pepper and onion. Pour the water around the roast. Bake, covered, at 350 degrees for 2½ hours.

Serves 4
Brenda Lanche, Riverside Branch

Ramekins Provençale

Great way to use leftover pot roast or roast beef.

2 cups (1½-inch) cubes leftover beef, poultry or
    a combination of beef and poultry
Salt and pepper to taste
3 tablespoons vegetable oil
1 medium onion, chopped
1 to 1½ cups boiling water
1 garlic clove
1 herb bouquet
Garlic cloves to taste
2 (16-ounce) cans pork and beans
8 ounces link sausage, sliced, browned
½ cup chili sauce, strained
½ cup buttered soft bread crumbs

Season the beef and/or poultry with salt and pepper. Cook in the hot oil in a skillet until brown on both sides; drain. Add the onion. Cook until the onion is golden brown. Add just enough of the boiling water to the skillet to cover the meat mixture. Add 1 garlic clove and herb bouquet. Simmer for 15 minutes, stirring occasionally. Discard the garlic and herb bouquet.

    Rub the insides of 4 to 6 ramekins with garlic. Spread 1 layer of beans in the ramekins. Top with a layer of sausage. Using a slotted spoon, spoon the beef or poultry over the top of the prepared layers and spread with another layer of beans.

    Stir the chili sauce into the remaining pan juices in the skillet and mix well. Drizzle the chili sauce mixture over the beans. Sprinkle with the bread crumbs. Bake at 350 degrees for 45 minutes.

    Tie sprigs of fresh parsley, fresh thyme, bay leaves and celery tops in cheesecloth to make your own herb bouquet, adding any of your favorite herbs as desired.

Serves 4 to 6
Connie Barnes, Watauga Public Library

Ramekin (RAM·ih·kihn)
Individual baking dish, 3 to 4 inches in diameter. Usually porcelain or earthenware.

My Mother's Brisket

1 tablespoon vegetable oil
1 (5- to 6-pound) first-cut beef brisket
Salt and pepper to taste
3 large yellow onions, cut into ½-inch pieces (about 3 pounds)
2 tablespoons vegetable oil
2 or 3 large garlic cloves, or to taste, minced
1 teaspoon Hungarian paprika
¾ teaspoon salt
¾ teaspoon freshly ground pepper
3 cups water

Pour 1 tablespoon oil into a Dutch oven or heavy baking pan large enough to hold the brisket. Heat the pan in a preheated 375-degree oven for 10 minutes. Pat the brisket dry with paper towels and sprinkle with salt and pepper. Add the brisket to the preheated Dutch oven. Roast for 30 minutes.

Cook the onions in 2 tablespoons oil in a large skillet over medium-high heat until tender and just beginning to brown, stirring constantly; reduce heat. Cook for 20 minutes longer or until the onions are golden brown, stirring occasionally and reducing the heat further if needed. Add the garlic, paprika, ¾ teaspoon salt and ¾ teaspoon pepper and mix well. Stir in the water. Bring to a boil, stirring occasionally.

Spoon the onion mixture over the brisket. Bake, with lid ½ inch ajar, for 3½ hours or until the brisket is tender. Check the brisket every hour, adding additional water if needed. Let the brisket stand in the onion mixture until cool.

Remove the brisket from the pan, scraping the onion mixture back into the Dutch oven. Wrap the brisket in foil. Chill for 8 to 10 hours. Spoon the onion mixture into a 1-quart container. Chill, covered, for 8 to 10 hours.

Discard the fat from the onion mixture. Combine the onion mixture with enough water to measure 3 cups. Pour into a blender container. Process until smooth. Pour the onion mixture into a large ovenproof skillet. Heat at 350 degrees until hot.

Slice the brisket against the grain to the desired thickness. Add the sliced brisket to the hot onion mixture. Heat for 30 minutes.

Serves 8 to 10
Sarah Harris, Riverside Branch

Mom's Flank Steak

This is a good way to serve steak to a family of six on a tight budget. If flank steak is not available substitute with skirt steak or London broil.

¼ cup (½ stick) margarine
1 teaspoon salt

¼ teaspoon dry mustard
1 (2-pound) beef flank steak

Heat the margarine in a large skillet until melted. Stir in the salt and dry mustard. Add the steak. Cook over medium-high heat until brown on both sides, turning once; do not overcook. Let stand for 5 to 10 minutes. Slice against the grain to the desired thickness.

Serves 6
Roberta Schenewerk, Central Library

Easy Beef Stroganoff

1 pound beef round steak, cut into
   chunks
Flour
1 tablespoon vegetable oil
½ cup chopped onion
1 garlic clove, crushed
1 (10-ounce) can tomato soup

1 (6-ounce) can mushrooms, drained
1 tablespoon Worcestershire sauce
½ teaspoon salt
6 to 8 drops of Tabasco sauce
Sour cream to taste
½ (7-ounce) package wide egg
   noodles, cooked, drained

Coat the beef with flour. Brown the beef on all sides in the oil in a skillet. Add the onion and garlic. Cook until the onion is tender, stirring frequently. Stir in the soup, mushrooms, Worcestershire sauce, salt and Tabasco sauce.

    Simmer over low heat for 45 minutes, stirring occasionally. Add the desired amount of sour cream and mix well. Spoon the beef mixture over the hot noodles on a serving platter.

Serves 4
Sarah Harris, Riverside Branch

Italian Steak and Sausage

This makes a great hot sandwich filling.

2 tablespoons flour
1 pound Italian sausage links, cut into 2-inch pieces
1 pound beef round steak, cut into 1/4-inch strips
1 (15-ounce) jar spaghetti sauce
2 cups sliced fresh mushrooms
1 green bell pepper, sliced
1 red bell pepper, sliced
1 medium onion, sliced
6 cups cooked white rice
Grated Parmesan cheese to taste

Shake the flour in a large oven-cooking bag. Place the bag in a
9×13-inch baking pan. Add the sausage, steak, spaghetti sauce,
mushrooms, bell peppers and onion to the bag. Squeeze the bag
gently to mix the ingredients and pat the contents into an even
layer. Seal tightly with a nylon tie.

Make six 1/2-inch slits in the top of the bag. Bake at 325 degrees
for 1 1/4 hours. Spoon the sausage mixture over the rice on a serving
platter. Sprinkle with cheese.

Serves 6
Roberta Schenewerk, Central Library

Swiss Steak

1 (2-pound) beef round steak
1/4 cup flour
3 tablespoons vegetable oil
1 1/2 teaspoons salt
1/2 teaspoon seasoned salt
1/4 teaspoon pepper
1 large onion, sliced
1 cup water
Hot cooked rice

Coat the steak on both sides with the flour. Brown the steak on both sides in the oil in a skillet over medium heat. Sprinkle the salt, seasoned salt and pepper over the steak. Add the onion and 1/2 cup of the water.

Simmer, covered, for 1 1/2 hours or until the steak is tender, stirring occasionally and adding the remaining 1/2 cup water during the cooking process. Spoon over hot cooked rice.

Serves 6
Brenda Lanche, Riverside Branch

Lazy Lou's Swiss Steak

This recipe started out very complicated. I shortened the steps using processed ingredients until I could put it together in no time. The cooking time allows time to bake potatoes as an accompaniment. This dish gives the appearance of a home-cooked meal that took hours to prepare.

1 (1 1/2-pound) beef round steak,
   3/4 inch thick
1 (15-ounce) can diced tomatoes
1 (10-ounce) can golden mushroom
   soup
1 tablespoon minced dried onion
Pepper to taste

Cut the steak into bite-size pieces. Brown the steak in a skillet sprayed with nonstick cooking spray. Combine the undrained tomatoes, soup, onion and pepper in a bowl and mix well. Add to the steak and mix well. Simmer, covered, for 1 1/2 hours, stirring occasionally.

Serves 4 to 6
Marion Edwards, Riverside Branch

Barbecued Ribs

1 cup ketchup
2 tablespoons minced onion
1 tablespoon liquid smoke
1 tablespoon Worcestershire sauce

2 teaspoons brown sugar
1/8 teaspoon Tabasco sauce
3 pounds beef ribs, cut into serving
portions

Combine the ketchup, onion, liquid smoke, Worcestershire sauce, brown sugar and Tabasco sauce in a large bowl and mix well. Dip the ribs in the sauce. Arrange the ribs in a large baking dish. Drizzle with the remaining sauce.

Bake, covered, at 300 degrees for 1 1/2 to 2 hours or until tender. Serve with mashed potatoes. Double the sauce ingredients if desired.

Serves 4
Brenda Lanche, Riverside Branch

Beef and Bean Goulash

2 pounds ground beef
2 large onions, thinly sliced
1 small bunch celery, chopped
2 garlic cloves, minced
2 (16-ounce) cans tomatoes
1 (16-ounce) can red kidney beans

1 (6-ounce) can tomato paste
1 (6-ounce) can mushrooms
2 teaspoons oregano
Green bell pepper, chopped (optional)
Salt and pepper to taste

Brown the ground beef in a skillet, stirring until crumbly; drain. Add the onions, celery and garlic to the ground beef and mix well. Simmer for 10 minutes, stirring constantly.

Spoon the ground beef mixture into a large saucepan or Dutch oven. Add the undrained tomatoes, undrained beans, tomato paste, undrained mushrooms, oregano, bell pepper, salt and pepper. Simmer, covered, for 2 to 3 hours or until of the desired consistency, stirring occasionally.

Serves 8
Dorothy Douglas, Haltom City Public Library

Beef Country Pie

CRUST
1 pound ground beef
1/2 cup bread crumbs
1/2 (8-ounce) can tomato sauce
1/4 cup chopped green bell pepper
1/4 cup chopped onion
1 1/2 teaspoons salt
1/8 teaspoon pepper
1/8 teaspoon oregano

RICE FILLING
1 1/3 cups instant rice
1 1/2 (8-ounce) cans tomato sauce
1 cup water
1 cup shredded cheese
1/2 teaspoon salt

For the crust, combine the ground beef, bread crumbs, tomato sauce, bell pepper, onion, salt, pepper and oregano in a bowl and mix well. Pat the ground beef mixture over the bottom and up the side of a greased 9-inch pie plate; flute the edge.

For the filling, combine the rice, tomato sauce, water, 1/4 cup of the cheese and salt in a bowl and mix well. Spoon the rice mixture into the prepared pie plate. Bake, covered with foil, at 350 degrees for 25 minutes. Remove the cover and sprinkle with the remaining 3/4 cup cheese. Bake for 10 minutes longer. Cut into wedges.

Serves 6 to 8
Cornelia Pim, Seminary South Branch

Growing Pains

In 1928, the need for additional space became critical; however, a bond issue to raise funds for a larger library failed, and the Library rented an annex at 209 1/2 Eighth Street to house a part of the growing collection.

(continued on page 70)

Black-Eyed Pea Casserole

This recipe originally came from my Aunt Lorene Plunkett. She brought this dish to a family reunion in 1983. My family especially enjoys it for our New Year's Day tradition of eating black-eyed peas for good luck. Of course, my northern friends can't believe we eat black-eyed peas in Texas. They use them as feed for their cows.

2 pounds ground beef
1 large onion, chopped
1 tablespoon Worcestershire sauce
1 teaspoon salt
1 teaspoon pepper
1/8 teaspoon garlic powder
2 (15-ounce) cans black-eyed peas with jalapeño chiles
1 (10-ounce) can tomatoes with chiles
1 (10-ounce) can cream of chicken soup
1 (10-ounce) can cream of mushroom soup
12 corn tortillas, torn, or tortilla chips
1 1/2 cups shredded Cheddar cheese

Brown the ground beef with the onion in a large skillet, stirring until the ground beef is crumbly; drain. Stir in the Worcestershire sauce, salt, pepper and garlic powder. Add the undrained black-eyed peas and undrained tomatoes and mix well.

Simmer for 10 minutes, stirring occasionally. Stir in the soups. Simmer for 10 minutes longer, stirring occasionally.

Line the bottom of a 9×13-inch baking dish with the torn tortillas. Spoon the ground beef mixture over the tortillas. Sprinkle with the cheese. Bake at 350 degrees for 20 minutes or until brown and bubbly.

Serves 6 to 8
Dianne Elrod, Haltom City Public Library

Black-eyed pea
A legume native to Asia, originally cultivated for animal fodder.

Ranch Bean Casserole

2 pounds lean ground beef
1 onion, chopped
1 (16-ounce) can ranch-style beans
1 can Spanish rice

Brown the ground beef with the onion in a large skillet, stirring until the ground beef is crumbly and the onion is tender; drain. Stir in the beans and rice. Bring to a boil, stirring frequently. Serve with crackers.

Serves 6 to 8
Brenda Groschup, Haltom City Public Library

Hamburger Sour Cream Casserole

1½ pounds ground beef
1 onion, chopped
1 green bell pepper, chopped
Salt and pepper to taste
3 cups cooked medium noodles
1 (10-ounce) can cream of chicken soup
1 (10-ounce) can cream of mushroom soup
1 (10-ounce) can corn niblets, drained
1 (2-ounce) jar chopped pimento, drained
1 cup sour cream
1 (5-ounce) can chow mein noodles

Brown the ground beef with the onion, bell pepper, salt and pepper in a skillet, stirring until the ground beef is crumbly; drain. Add the cooked noodles, soups, corn and pimento and mix well. Stir in the sour cream.

Spoon the ground beef mixture into a baking dish. Sprinkle with the chow mein noodles. Bake at 350 degrees for 1 hour. May freeze, covered, before baking for future use. Sprinkle with the chow mein noodles just before baking.

Serves 10
Dorothy Douglas, Haltom City Public Library

Hamburger *!?*!?

This recipe was concocted when I had planned to make beef stroganoff and discovered I did not have enough sour cream, as well as a few other ingredients. I did discover leftover sour cream, cottage cheese and cream cheese in the refrigerator. The ingredient amounts may be adjusted to suit your family's taste or the availability of ingredients in the refrigerator.

2 pounds ground beef
2 (8-ounce) cans tomato sauce
3 small onions, chopped
1 cup chopped celery
1 tablespoon salt
1 tablespoon sugar
3 garlic cloves, crushed, or the equivalent amount of garlic powder
1/4 teaspoon oregano
Pepper to taste
8 ounces cream cheese with chives, softened
1 cup cottage cheese
1 cup sour cream
12 to 16 ounces egg noodles, cooked, drained
1 1/2 cups shredded sharp Cheddar cheese

Brown the ground beef in a skillet, stirring until crumbly; drain. Stir in the tomato sauce, onions, celery, salt, sugar, garlic, oregano and pepper. Simmer, covered, for 15 to 20 minutes, stirring occasionally. Combine the cream cheese, cottage cheese and sour cream in a bowl and mix well.

Layer the noodles, cream cheese mixture and ground beef mixture 1/2 at a time in a baking dish. Sprinkle with the Cheddar cheese. Bake at 350 degrees for 25 to 30 minutes or until brown and bubbly.

Serves 6 to 8
Pat Jermyn, Richland Hills Public Library

Biscuit-Topped Italian Casserole

1 pound ground beef
½ cup chopped onion
1 (8-ounce) can tomato sauce
1 (6-ounce) can tomato paste
¾ cup water
¼ teaspoon pepper
1 (9-ounce) package frozen mixed vegetables, thawed
2 cups shredded mozzarella cheese
1 (10-count) can buttermilk biscuits
1 tablespoon butter or margarine, melted
½ teaspoon oregano, crushed

Brown the ground beef with the onion in a skillet, stirring until the ground beef is crumbly; drain. Stir in the tomato sauce, tomato paste, water and pepper. Simmer for 15 minutes, stirring occasionally. Remove from heat. Stir in the mixed vegetables and 1½ cups of the cheese. Spoon the ground beef mixture into a greased 8×12-inch baking dish.

Separate the 10 biscuits. Split each biscuit into halves. Arrange the biscuit halves slightly overlapping around the outer edge of the baking dish. Sprinkle the remaining ½ cup cheese over the center of the ground beef mixture. Brush the biscuits with the butter and sprinkle with the oregano. Bake at 375 degrees for 22 to 27 minutes or until the biscuits are golden brown.

Serves 4 to 6
Martha Carter, Central Library

Oregano (oh·REHG·uh·noh)
The Greek word for "joy of the mountain," oregano was introduced to the United States by soldiers returning from Italian World War II assignments.

Easy Lasagna

1 pound ground beef
1 onion, chopped
2 (8-ounce) cans tomato sauce
½ cup water
1 envelope spaghetti seasoning mix
1 to 2 cups cottage cheese
1 egg, beaten
¼ teaspoon nutmeg
6 to 8 ounces lasagna noodles, cooked, drained
8 ounces Cheddar cheese, shredded
8 ounces mozzarella cheese, shredded

Brown the ground beef with the onion in a skillet, stirring until
the ground beef is crumbly; drain. Stir in the tomato sauce, water
and seasoning mix. Simmer, covered, for 10 minutes, stirring
occasionally. Combine the cottage cheese, egg and nutmeg in a
bowl and mix well.

Layer the noodles, ground beef mixture and cottage cheese
mixture ½ at a time in a 9×13-inch baking pan. Sprinkle with a
mixture of the Cheddar cheese and mozzarella cheese. Bake at
350 degrees for 35 to 40 minutes or until brown and bubbly.

Serves 6 to 8
Karen Brown, Central Library

Pastitsio

GROUND BEEF FILLING

2 cups chopped onions
2 tablespoons butter
1 pound ground beef
1 (16-ounce) can whole tomatoes,
    drained, mashed
1 (8-ounce) can tomato sauce
3/4 teaspoon salt
1/2 teaspoon oregano
1/4 teaspoon cinnamon
1/8 teaspoon pepper
3 tablespoons bread crumbs
1 egg white, beaten

WHITE SAUCE AND ASSEMBLY

3 tablespoons butter
1/3 cup flour
2 1/2 cups milk
1 1/2 teaspoons salt
1/4 teaspoon nutmeg
1/8 teaspoon white pepper
3 eggs
1 egg yolk
1/2 cup ricotta cheese
3 tablespoons bread crumbs
8 ounces elbow macaroni, cooked,
    drained
1 cup grated Romano cheese

For the filling, sauté the onions in the butter in a skillet. Add the ground beef. Cook until the ground beef is brown and crumbly, stirring constantly; drain. Stir in the tomatoes, tomato sauce, salt, oregano, cinnamon and pepper. Simmer, covered, for 40 minutes, stirring occasionally. Let stand until cool. Stir in the bread crumbs and egg white.

For the sauce, heat the butter in a saucepan until melted. Stir in the flour. Cook over medium heat until smooth and bubbly, stirring constantly. Add the milk, salt, nutmeg and white pepper gradually, stirring constantly. Bring to a boil, stirring constantly. Boil for 1 minute, stirring constantly.

Whisk the eggs and egg yolk lightly in a bowl. Stir a small amount of the hot mixture into the eggs. Add the remaining white sauce to the eggs gradually, stirring constantly. Combine 1 cup of the white sauce and ricotta cheese in a bowl and mix well.

To assemble, sprinkle the bottom of a buttered 9×13-inch baking dish with bread crumbs. Spread with 1/2 of the pasta and cover with the ground beef filling. Sprinkle with 1/2 cup of the Romano cheese. Top with the remaining pasta. Bake at 350 degrees for 30 minutes. Remove from oven. Increase the oven temperature to 400 degrees. Layer with the ricotta cheese mixture and white sauce. Sprinkle with the remaining 1/2 cup Romano cheese. Bake for 30 minutes longer. Let stand for 10 minutes before serving.

Serves 6 to 8
Sarah Harris, Riverside Branch

Taleroni

My mother, Chris Flannagan, prepared this dish when I was growing up. Just add a salad and corn bread for a very satisfying meal. I always wondered where the name originated. It seemed to me that the "roni" meant that the original ingredient might have been macaroni. My mother may have substituted the noodles to shorten the cooking time. I have the baking dish she used and remember the crusty edges of the casserole which resulted when we were really hungry and increased the oven temperature to hurry supper.

1 pound ground beef
1 (15-ounce) can whole peeled
   tomatoes
1 (8-ounce) can tomato sauce, or
   2 (6-ounce) cans tomato paste

1 small onion, chopped
1/2 package small egg noodles
1 teaspoon salt
1 (16-ounce) can corn, drained
8 ounces Cheddar cheese, shredded

Brown the ground beef in a large skillet, stirring until crumbly; drain. Add the undrained tomatoes, tomato sauce, onion, pasta and salt. Cook until the pasta is tender, stirring frequently. Remove from heat. Stir in the corn and cheese. Spoon the ground beef mixture into a baking dish. Bake at 350 degrees for 30 to 45 minutes or until bubbly. Leftovers are great reheated.

Serves 2 to 4
Dianne Elrod, Haltom City Public Library

Chunk O' Cheese Meat Loaf

Cool the meat loaf for thirty minutes before slicing to reveal the cheese chunks throughout the loaf. May substitute pork or veal for the ground beef.

1 1/2 pounds ground beef
4 ounces fresh mushrooms, chopped
1 medium onion, chopped
3/4 cup dry bread crumbs
3/4 cup milk
1/4 cup minced fresh parsley

1 egg, lightly beaten
1 1/2 teaspoons salt
1/2 teaspoon pepper
8 ounces extra-sharp Cheddar cheese,
   cut into 1/2-inch cubes

Mix all the ingredients except the cheese in a bowl. Add the cheese and mix until evenly distributed. Shape into a loaf and place in a baking pan. Bake at 350 degrees for 1 to 1 1/2 hours or until cooked through; drain.

Serves 6 to 8
Corina Escamilla, Wedgwood Branch

Salisbury Steak

1½ pounds ground beef
1 (10-ounce) can onion soup
½ cup fine dry bread crumbs
1 egg, lightly beaten
⅛ teaspoon pepper

¼ cup ketchup
1 teaspoon Worcestershire sauce
½ teaspoon prepared mustard
1 tablespoon flour

Combine the ground beef, ⅓ cup of the soup, bread crumbs, egg and pepper in a bowl and mix well. Shape the ground beef mixture into 6 oval patties. Brown the patties on both sides in a skillet sprayed with nonstick cooking spray; drain.

Combine the remaining soup, ketchup, Worcestershire sauce and prepared mustard in a bowl and mix well. Combine the flour with just enough water in a bowl until of a smooth consistency. Stir the flour mixture into the soup mixture. Pour the soup mixture over the patties in the skillet. Cook, covered, over low heat for 20 minutes or until the patties are cooked through, stirring occasionally.

Serves 6
Marion Edwards, Riverside Branch

Spaghettilicious

2½ pounds ground beef
1 onion, chopped
1 bell pepper, chopped
1½ tablespoons salt, or to taste
1 tablespoon pepper, or to taste
2 (16-ounce) packages beef sausage
   links, cut into bite-size pieces

1 (26-ounce) jar spaghetti sauce
1 tablespoon garlic salt
24 to 32 ounces thin spaghetti,
   cooked, drained
8 ounces Cheddar cheese, shredded

Brown the ground beef with the onion, bell pepper, salt and pepper in a large skillet, stirring until the ground beef is crumbly; drain. Brown the sausage in a skillet; drain. Stir the sausage into the ground beef mixture. Add the spaghetti sauce and garlic salt and mix well. Simmer until of the desired consistency, stirring occasionally. Add the spaghetti and mix well. Spoon into a serving bowl. Sprinkle with the cheese. Serve immediately with garlic bread.

Serves 6 to 8
Arlon Taylor, Wedgwood Branch

Enchilada Casserole

2 pounds ground beef
1 large onion, chopped
1 (28-ounce) can tomatoes
1 (10-ounce) package frozen chopped spinach, cooked, drained
Salt and pepper to taste
1 (10-ounce) can cream of mushroom soup
1 (10-ounce) can golden mushroom soup
1 to 2 cups sour cream
1/4 cup milk
1/4 teaspoon garlic powder
12 to 16 corn tortillas
1/2 cup (1 stick) butter, melted
1 (4-ounce) can chopped green chiles, drained
8 ounces longhorn cheese, shredded

Brown the ground beef with the onion in a large skillet, stirring until the ground beef is crumbly; drain. Stir in the undrained tomatoes, spinach, salt and pepper. Remove from heat.

Combine the soups, sour cream, milk and garlic powder in a bowl and mix well. Dip 1/2 of the tortillas in the melted butter and arrange overlapping over the bottom of a 9×13-inch baking pan. Spread with the ground beef mixture. Sprinkle with the green chiles and 1/2 of the cheese. Top with 1/2 of the soup mixture.

Dip the remaining tortillas in the melted butter and arrange over the top of the prepared layers. Top with the remaining soup mixture and remaining cheese. Cover and let stand for 5 minutes at room temperature. Bake at 325 degrees for 35 to 45 minutes or until bubbly.

Serves 6 to 8
Faye Turner, Butler Outreach Library Division

Green Enchiladas

2 pounds lean ground beef
1 onion, chopped
1 (10-ounce) can cream of mushroom
   soup
1 (10-ounce) can cream of chicken
   soup

1 (10-ounce) can Cheddar cheese soup
1 (10-ounce) can diced tomatoes with
   chiles
1 (4-ounce) can chopped green chiles
1 can (12-ounce) evaporated milk
1 large package Doritos

Brown the ground beef with the onion in a skillet, stirring until the ground beef is crumbly; drain. Add the soups, undrained tomatoes, green chiles and evaporated milk and mix well.

Arrange the chips over the bottom of a large baking dish. Spoon the ground beef mixture over the chips. Bake at 400 degrees for 40 minutes.

Serves 6 to 8
Brenda Groschup, Haltom City Public Library

Quick Mexican Pizza

8 ounces ground beef
1½ teaspoons chili powder
½ teaspoon cumin
4 (10-inch) flour tortillas
1 cup salsa

2 cups shredded Colby-Jack cheese
Chopped green and red bell peppers
Chopped onion
Sliced mushrooms

Brown the ground beef in a skillet, stirring until crumbly; drain. Stir in the chili powder and cumin. Arrange the tortillas on a baking sheet. Spread each with ¼ cup of the salsa and ½ cup of the ground beef mixture. Sprinkle each with ½ cup of the cheese, bell peppers, onion and mushrooms. Bake at 400 degrees for 8 to 10 minutes or until light brown and bubbly. May vary toppings as desired.

Serves 4
Karen Brown, Central Library

Pizza Burgers

4 pounds ground beef
3 pounds bulk pork sausage
1 large onion, grated
2 (12-ounce) cans tomato paste
1 teaspoon garlic salt
1 teaspoon red pepper flakes

1 teaspoon oregano
1½ pounds mozzarella cheese,
  shredded
1 pound Cheddar cheese, shredded
1 pound Swiss cheese, shredded
36 English muffins, split

Brown the ground beef and sausage with the onion in a large skillet, stirring until the ground beef and sausage are crumbly; drain. Stir in the tomato paste, garlic salt, red pepper flakes and oregano. Cook, covered, for 10 minutes, stirring occasionally. Combine the mozzarella cheese, Cheddar cheese and Swiss cheese in a bowl and mix well.

Spread each muffin half with about ¼ cup of the ground beef mixture. Sprinkle each with a generous amount of the cheese mixture. Arrange in a single layer on a baking sheet. Freeze until firm.

Store the pizza burgers in sealable plastic freezer bags. Heat the frozen pizzas on a baking sheet at 350 degrees for 25 to 30 minutes or until brown and bubbly.

Makes 72 pizza burgers
Connie Sullivan, Keller Public Library

Sloppy Joes

1 pound ground beef
½ cup chopped onion
¼ cup chopped celery
¼ cup chopped green bell pepper
1 (8-ounce) can tomato sauce
¼ cup ketchup

1 tablespoon sugar
1 tablespoon vinegar
1½ teaspoons Worcestershire sauce
1 teaspoon salt
⅛ teaspoon pepper
6 to 8 hamburger buns

Brown the ground beef with the onion, celery and bell pepper in a skillet, stirring until the ground beef is crumbly; drain. Stir in the tomato sauce, ketchup, sugar, vinegar, Worcestershire sauce, salt and pepper. Simmer for 1 hour, stirring occasionally. Serve on hamburger buns.

Serves 6 to 8
Betty Howe, Keller Public Library

Chili Rice Casserole

1 (19-ounce) can chili
3 cups cooked rice
1 cup shredded Cheddar cheese
1/2 cup chopped onion
3/4 cup crushed corn chips

Heat the chili in a saucepan, stirring occasionally. Remove from heat. Spread the rice in a lightly greased 9×9-inch baking dish. Layer with 1/2 of the cheese and 1/2 of the onion. Spread with the chili. Top with the remaining cheese and remaining onion. Sprinkle with the corn chips. Bake at 375 degrees for 25 to 30 minutes or until bubbly.

Serves 6
Karen Brown, Central Library

Frito Chili Pie

1 large package regular Fritos
1 to 3 (19-ounce) cans chili with or without beans
Shredded Cheddar cheese to taste
Chopped onion to taste

Cover the bottom of an electric skillet with Fritos. Spoon the chili over the chips. Sprinkle with cheese and onion. Heat, covered, until the cheese melts and the chili is hot. You may add as many layers of Fritos and chili as you desire.

Serves 4 to 6
Karen Brown, Central Library

Take a Byte

In 1984, Cate Dixon, Assistant Director, was hired to begin the library automation, featuring a computerized catalog. The project was completed in 1986.

Mediterranean Pork Roast

1 (3-pound) boneless pork roast, tied
1 (15-ounce) can tomato sauce
1 (15-ounce) can pitted black olives, drained, chopped
1 onion, grated
½ cup golden raisins
¼ cup vinegar
1 tablespoon brown sugar
Capers to taste

Place the roast in a shallow baking pan or dish. Combine the tomato sauce, olives, onion, raisins, vinegar, brown sugar and capers in a bowl and mix well. Pour the tomato sauce mixture over the roast. Insert a meat thermometer in the roast.

Bake at 325 to 350 degrees for 2 to 3 hours or until a meat thermometer registers 170 degrees.

Serves 6 to 8
Sarah Harris, Riverside Branch

Baked Pork Chops

8 center-cut pork chops
Salt and pepper to taste
8 thin lemon slices
½ cup packed brown sugar
1 (32-ounce) bottle ketchup
4 cups water

Season the pork chops with salt and pepper. Arrange in a single layer in a baking dish. Top each pork chop with 1 lemon slice. Spread each with 1 tablespoon of the brown sugar. Bake at 325 degrees until the chops are brown and the brown sugar is melted.

Combine the ketchup and water in a bowl and mix well. Pour over the pork chops. Bake, covered, until the pork chops are cooked through and the sauce has thickened.

Serves 8
Doris Snider, Haltom City Public Library

Mushroom Pork Chops

4 pork chops, trimmed
Vegetable oil
1 (10-ounce) can cream of mushroom soup
1/4 cup water
1/8 teaspoon garlic salt

Brown the pork chops in oil in a skillet; drain. Add the soup, water and garlic salt and mix well. Simmer over low heat for 45 minutes or until the pork chops are tender, stirring occasionally.

Serves 4
Brenda Lanche, Riverside Branch

Sweet-and-Sour Spareribs

3 pounds spareribs, cut into serving portions
Salt and pepper to taste
1 cup crushed pineapple with juice
2/3 cup packed brown sugar
2/3 cup vinegar
1/2 cup ketchup
1/2 cup water
1/4 cup chopped green bell pepper
2 tablespoons soy sauce
2 tablespoons cornstarch
2 teaspoons dry mustard

Arrange the spareribs meat side up in a single layer in a large shallow baking pan. Bake at 425 degrees for 20 to 30 minutes or until brown; drain. Sprinkle with salt and pepper.
Combine the pineapple, brown sugar, vinegar, ketchup, water, bell pepper, soy sauce, cornstarch and dry mustard in a saucepan and mix well. Cook over medium heat until thickened and glossy and of sauce consistency, stirring constantly. Pour the pineapple mixture over the ribs. Bake, covered or uncovered, at 350 degrees for 1 hour.

Serves 6
Brenda Lanche, Riverside Branch

Sausage Jambalaya

1 teaspoon vegetable oil
1 pound sausage, sliced
1 cup chopped onion
1 cup chopped celery
1 cup chopped bell pepper
2 garlic cloves, finely chopped
1/2 teaspoon salt
1/8 teaspoon thyme
1/8 teaspoon cayenne pepper
8 to 16 ounces deveined peeled shrimp (optional)
1 1/2 cups rice
3 cups water

Heat a 4-quart stockpot over medium-high heat. Add the oil. Brown the sausage in the hot oil; drain. Add the onion, celery and bell pepper and mix well. Sauté until the onion is tender. Stir in the garlic, salt, thyme and cayenne pepper. Add the shrimp. Cook until the shrimp turn pink, stirring constantly. Add the rice and water. Bring to a boil; reduce heat. Simmer, covered, for 45 minutes, stirring occasionally. Ladle into bowls.

Serves 4 to 6
Cydney Nida, Haltom City Public Library

Jambalaya (juhm·buh·LI·yah)
It is thought the name of this Creole dish derives from the French word *jambon* (ham), frequently the main ingredient.

Baked Pasta Casserole

16 ounces mostaccioli, ziti or rotini
1 pound bulk Italian sausage or lean ground beef
2 (26-ounce) jars ripe olive and mushroom pasta sauce or
    tomato and basil pasta sauce
4 cups shredded mozzarella cheese
Chopped fresh parsley

Prepare the desired pasta in a saucepan using package directions; drain. Brown the sausage in a skillet, stirring until the sausage is, crumbly; drain.

Combine the pasta, sausage, pasta sauce and 2 cups of the cheese in a bowl and mix well. Spoon the pasta mixture into a greased 9×13-inch baking dish. Bake, covered, at 350 degrees for 45 minutes or until bubbly; remove cover. Sprinkle with the remaining 2 cups cheese and parsley. Bake for 10 minutes longer or until the cheese melts.

May substitute a mixture of 8 ounces sausage and 8 ounces ground beef for the sausage or ground beef.

Serves 6 to 8
Martha Carter, Central Library

Pineapple, Ham and Rice Casserole

Great way to use leftover ham.

1 (20-ounce) can crushed pineapple
2 cups cooked rice
2 cups cubed cooked ham
½ cup packed brown sugar
1 tablespoon lemon juice
1 teaspoon dry mustard

Combine the undrained pineapple, rice, ham, brown sugar, lemon juice and dry mustard in a bowl and mix well. Spoon the ham mixture into a greased 1½-quart baking dish. Bake at 350 degrees for 25 to 30 minutes or until heated through.

Serves 4
Sylvia Autrey, Wedgwood Branch

Bacon Spaghetti

2 pounds country-style bacon, chopped
1 onion, chopped
2 (28-ounce) cans tomatoes
1 or 2 dried red peppers, chopped
16 ounces spaghetti, cooked, drained

Fry the bacon and onion in a skillet until the bacon is brown and crisp; drain. Stir in the undrained tomatoes and red peppers. Simmer until of the desired consistency, stirring occasionally. Combine the bacon mixture and hot spaghetti in a pasta bowl and mix gently. Serve immediately.

Serves 6 to 8
Betty Patterson, Richland Hills Public Library

ENTREES
CHICKEN, SEAFOOD & VEGETARIAN

sea·food (sē′fo͞od′) n.

Fish or shellfish such as Salmon or shrimp,
used as food.

Shown above: Fort Worth Public Library, Art Gallery, 1939-1978

A Tornado Strikes

On March 28, 2000, a tornado hit dowtown Fort Worth damaging many buildings, including the Central Library. Meteorologists reported that the tornado did so much damage because it stayed on the ground for 15 to 30 minutes. The Central Library sustained $1.2 million in damage as the winds blew through the building scattering the contents.

(continued on page 88)

Chicken à la Grecque

1 tablespoon oregano
½ teaspoon salt
¼ teaspoon freshly ground pepper
1 (3-pound) chicken, cut up
¼ cup olive oil
2 tablespoons lemon juice

Combine the oregano, salt and pepper in a small bowl and mix well. Rub the seasoning mixture over the surface of the chicken. Arrange the chicken in a single layer in a 9×13-inch baking dish. Drizzle with a mixture of the olive oil and lemon juice. Bake at 400 degrees for 40 minutes or until the chicken is cooked through.

Serves 4 or 5
Pearlie Miller, East Berry Branch

No-Peek Chicken and Rice

¼ cup (½ stick) margarine, cut into chunks
1 cup rice
2 cups water
1 (3-pound) chicken, cut up
1 envelope onion soup mix

Layer the margarine, rice, water and chicken in a 9×13-inch baking dish. Sprinkle with the soup mix. Bake, covered with foil, at 325 degrees for 70 minutes; do not "peek." May substitute your favorite chicken pieces for the whole chicken.

Serves 4 or 5
Gerry Humphreys, Wedgwood Branch

Chicken Enchiladas

1 (3-pound) chicken, cooked
Mild to hot salsa to taste
1 small onion, chopped
1 to 2 tablespoons butter

2 cups shredded Monterey Jack
 cheese
8 to 10 flour tortillas

Chop the chicken, discarding the skin and bones. Spread the desired amount of salsa over the bottom of a 9×9-inch baking dish. Sauté the onion in the butter in a skillet until tender. Stir in the chicken, desired amount of salsa and 1 cup of the cheese.

Spoon some of the chicken mixture in the center of each tortilla. Roll to enclose the filling. Arrange the tortillas seam side down in the prepared baking dish. Spread with the desired amount of salsa and sprinkle with the remaining 1 cup cheese. Bake at 350 degrees for 20 minutes or until the cheese melts.

Serves 8 to 10
Ann Gray Rethard, Haltom City Public Library

Chicken Spaghetti

This recipe is dedicated to the memory of Reen Jones, who was a very good cook.

3 large green bell peppers, chopped
3 large onions, chopped
1½ cups sliced celery
Butter
2 (16-ounce) cans tomatoes, partially
 drained
1 hen or 2 large fryers, cooked, boned,
 chopped

1 pound processed cheese, shredded
1 pound sharp Cheddar cheese,
 shredded
2 (10-ounce) cans cream of mushroom
 soup
Salt and pepper to taste
2 to 3 cups spaghetti, cooked

Sauté the bell peppers, onions and celery in butter in a Dutch oven until brown. Add the partially drained tomatoes and mix well. Simmer for 20 minutes, stirring occasionally. Stir in the chicken, cheese, soup, salt and pepper. Cook until heated through, stirring frequently. Layer the spaghetti and chicken mixture ½ at a time in 1 or 2 baking pans sprayed with nonstick cooking spray.

Bake at 350 degrees for 20 minutes. The chicken mixture may be prepared and frozen for future use. Thaw just before baking and layer with the spaghetti. May substitute leftover turkey for the chicken. Cut the recipe in half for a smaller crowd.

Serves 12 to 15
Karen Brown, Central Library

Mama's Chicken and Rice

Of all my mother's casserole recipes, this is my favorite. I have tried to make it taste just like she did and can't quite achieve that perfect taste. My sister Rita can come real close. It is funny how there are tastes that we can remember but can't recreate.

1 (3-pound) chicken, cut up, or
   6 boneless skinless chicken breasts
Flour
1/2 teaspoon garlic powder (optional)
Salt and pepper to taste
1 onion, chopped

1 (10-ounce) can each cream of
   mushroom and cream of chicken
   soup
1 (2-ounce) jar chopped pimento,
   drained
3 cups cooked rice

Coat the chicken with flour. Sprinkle with the garlic powder, salt and pepper. Combine the chicken and onion in a nonstick skillet. Cook, covered, until the chicken and onion are tender, turning occasionally; remove cover. Cook until the chicken is brown on both sides. Remove the chicken to a platter with a slotted spoon. Drain most of the pan drippings.
   Stir the soups and pimento into the reserved pan drippings and mix well. Stir in the rice. Spoon the rice mixture into a 9×13-inch baking dish. Add the chicken and mix until the chicken is covered with the rice mixture. Bake, covered, at 350 degrees for 30 minutes or until the chicken falls from the bone or is cooked through.

Serves 4 or 5
Brenda Lanche, Riverside Branch

Baked Chicken Breasts

This is a "souper" recipe to cook after a hard day at the office. Serve with instant mashed potatoes, a frozen vegetable, and salad in a bag.

4 chicken breasts
Meat tenderizer
1 (10-ounce) can cream of chicken
   mushroom soup

1/2 soup can water
Chopped pimento

Sprinkle the chicken with meat tenderizer. Arrange in a single layer in an ungreased baking dish. Pour a mixture of the soup and water over the chicken. Top with the pimento. Bake at 350 degrees for 1 hour or until the chicken is cooked through.

Serves 4
Marion Edwards, Riverside Branch

Smothered Chicken

½ cup flour
1 tablespoon sage
1 tablespoon poultry seasoning
Salt and pepper to taste
1 (2½- to 3-pound) chicken, cut up

1 cup olive or vegetable oil
1 (10-ounce) can cream of mushroom
  soup
1½ cups water
1 medium onion, sliced

Combine the flour, sage, poultry seasoning, salt and pepper in a shallow dish and mix well. Coat the chicken with the flour mixture. Brown the chicken on all sides in the olive oil in a large heavy skillet. Remove the chicken to a platter with a slotted spoon, reserving the pan drippings. Add the remaining flour mixture to the reserved pan drippings and mix well.

Cook until golden brown, stirring constantly. Add the soup and water gradually, stirring constantly. Return the chicken to the skillet. Add the onion. Cook, covered, over low heat for 25 to 30 minutes or until the chicken is cooked through, stirring occasionally.

Serves 4
Karen Brown, Central Library

Tater-Dipped Chicken

This was a family favorite when I was growing up. Being more diet-conscious I seldom prepare this dish anymore. Occasionally, when all my sisters get together, we just have to give in to the urge and prepare this dish. This is a Robbins' family comfort food and it is just not the same with boneless skinless chicken breasts.

1 egg, lightly beaten
2 tablespoons water
Salt and pepper to taste

1 (3-pound) chicken, cut up
1 cup instant potato flakes
¼ cup (½ stick) margarine

Whisk the egg, water, salt and pepper in a bowl. Dip the chicken in the egg mixture and coat with the potato flakes. Heat the margarine in a shallow baking pan until melted. Arrange the chicken skin side down in the butter. Bake at 400 degrees for 1 hour, turning once.

Serves 6
Roberta Schenewerk, Central Library

Doors and windows were blown out, the air conditioning system was severely damaged, and one unit was blown away. The rare books section of the Genealogy/Local History/City Archives had extensive water damage. The newly opened Hazel Peace Youth Center had extensive glass breakage and flooding. Workers were kept busy removing glass particles from book jackets and computer keyboards.

(continued on page 91)

Chicken à la Sampion

16 ounces small pasta shells
Salt to taste
8 slices bacon
8 boneless skinless chicken breasts
4 cups sour cream
2 (10-ounce) cans cream of mushroom soup
1 (8-ounce) can artichoke quarters, drained
Chopped mushrooms to taste
1/2 teaspoon marjoram
1/2 teaspoon tarragon
1/2 teaspoon salt

Cook the pasta in boiling salted water in a saucepan for 10 to 12 minutes or until al dente; drain. Cook the bacon in a large skillet over low heat until tender but not crisp. Remove the bacon to paper towels to drain, reserving 1/4 cup of the bacon drippings.

Pound the chicken 1/4 inch thick between sheets of waxed paper with a meat mallet. Cook the chicken in the reserved bacon drippings over medium heat for 4 minutes per side or just until light brown. Remove the chicken with a slotted spoon to a platter. Wrap each chicken breast with 1 slice of the bacon; secure with wooden picks.

Combine the sour cream, soup, artichokes, mushrooms, marjoram, tarragon and 1/2 teaspoon salt in a saucepan and mix well. Cook over low heat until heated through, stirring constantly. Remove from heat.

Place the pasta in a disposable 12×14-inch roasting pan. Add 1/3 of the sour cream mixture and mix well. Arrange the chicken over the prepared layer. Spread with the remaining sour cream mixture. Bake, covered with foil, at 350 degrees for 45 minutes or until the chicken is cooked through.

Serves 8
Pearlie Miller, East Berry Branch

Chicken Cacciatore

Another of Jim Barnes' creations that works very well. He has no idea of the exact measurements of the ingredients he chooses to use, but I have done a "best guess" for those who prefer to follow a recipe. Jim claims he justs puts in the amount that feels right.

4 chicken breasts
2 tablespoons olive oil
1 onion, sliced
Fresh tomatoes, blanched, peeled, chopped, or
   canned chopped tomatoes
Red bell pepper, sliced
Fresh mushrooms, sliced
1 or 2 garlic cloves, minced
Fresh or dried basil
Balsamic vinegar, cooking wine or your favorite wine to taste
1 to 2 teaspoons sugar (optional)
Salt and pepper to taste

Brown the chicken on both sides in the olive oil in a skillet. Remove the chicken to a platter with a slotted spoon, reserving the pan drippings. Sauté the onion in the reserved pan drippings. Stir in the tomatoes, bell pepper, mushrooms, garlic and basil. Return the chicken to the skillet. Stir in the desired amount of balsamic vinegar. Simmer over low heat until the chicken is cooked through, stirring occasionally. Add the sugar, salt and pepper and mix well.

The balsamic vinegar adds a sweetness to the recipe that we like, so you may prefer to omit the sugar. The cooking wine is salty, as are the canned tomatoes, so adjust the salt accordingly. The balsamic vinegar, cooking wine or your favorite wine will add a richness and tenderness to the dish.

Serves 4
Connie Barnes, Watauga Public Library

Cacciatore (kah·cha·TOR·ee)
Italian word for hunter. A dish prepared with mushrooms, onions, tomatoes, herbs, and sometimes wine.

Cyd's Chicken Curry

My four children are grown, but when they were young we would celebrate other cultures by preparing foods of various countries. Sometimes we would decorate the table accordingly. This was a learning experience for all.

1 onion, minced
1 rib celery, minced
1 large apple, peeled, chopped
2 tablespoons butter
1¼ tablespoons curry powder
½ cup chicken broth
1 quart half-and-half
¼ cup cold water
2 tablespoons cornstarch
4 boneless skinless chicken breasts, cooked, cut into halves
Hot cooked rice
Paprika to taste

Sauté the onion, celery and apple in the butter in a skillet until the onion is tender. Stir in the curry powder. Add the broth and mix well. Simmer for 5 minutes, stirring occasionally. Stir in the half-and-half.

Combine the water and cornstarch in a small bowl and mix well. Stir the cornstarch mixture into the broth mixture. Cook until of the desired thickness, stirring constantly.

Add the chicken to the skillet and mix well. Simmer until heated through, stirring occasionally. Spoon the chicken and sauce over hot cooked rice on a serving platter. Sprinkle with paprika. Serve with a salad or sliced cucumbers. Fill small cups with shredded coconut, raisins, slivered almonds, chopped peanuts or pine nuts for additional toppings.

Serves 4
Cydney Nida, Haltom City Public Library

Curry
A hot, spicy dish of East Indian origin, flavored with curry powder.

Chicken Poblano Enchiladas

3 pounds boneless skinless chicken breasts
3 fresh poblano chiles, roasted, seeded, chopped
1 large tomato, chopped
½ cup chopped onion
3 garlic cloves, minced
1 teaspoon cumin
½ teaspoon salt
½ cup chicken broth
1½ cups heavy cream
12 corn tortillas
2 cups shredded Monterey Jack cheese
Chopped red bell pepper

Combine the chicken, poblano chiles, tomato, onion, garlic, cumin and salt in a skillet and mix well. Add the broth. Bring to a boil over medium heat; reduce heat. Simmer for 1 hour, stirring occasionally. Remove the chicken with a slotted spoon to a platter. Cool the chicken slightly and shred. Spoon the poblano chile mixture into a 9×13-inch baking dish.

Heat the heavy cream in a saucepan. Remove from heat. Add the tortillas. Let stand until soft. Spoon some of the shredded chicken in the center of each tortilla. Roll to enclose the filling. Arrange the tortillas seam side down in the prepared baking dish. Pour the remaining warm cream over the tortillas. Sprinkle with the cheese and bell pepper. Bake at 375 degrees for 25 minutes or until heated through.

Makes 12 enchiladas
Brenda McCrary, Richland Hills Public Library

Tornado, continued

In addition to supporting the Central Library during the time it was closed for repairs, the Branches assisted the City by sorting through trash bags full of documents which had been blown from the nearby office buildings and scattered by the high winds. The torn, muddied, and wadded-up papers were sorted, and phone calls were made to the names and businesses identified on the documents in an effort to return them to their owners.

Creole Chicken and Shrimp with Linguini

2 tablespoons butter or margarine
1 tablespoon vegetable oil
1¼ to 1½ ponds boneless skinless chicken breasts,
    cut into ½-inch pieces
1 pound shrimp, peeled, deveined
1 teaspoon oregano
½ teaspoon salt
¼ teaspoon freshly ground black pepper
¼ teaspoon cayenne pepper
2 tablespoons butter
1 tablespoon vegetable oil
1 onion, chopped
1 green bell pepper, chopped
2 garlic cloves, crushed
1 tomato, peeled, chopped
2 tablespoons Worcestershire sauce
2 tablespoons lemon juice
16 ounces linguini, cooked, drained

Heat 2 tablespoons butter and 1 tablespoon oil in a large skillet over medium-high heat. Add the chicken and shrimp and mix well. Sprinkle with the oregano, salt, black pepper and cayenne pepper.

Sauté for 3 minutes or until the chicken is cooked through and the shrimp turn pink. Remove the chicken and shrimp to a bowl with a slotted spoon, reserving the pan drippings. Reduce the heat to medium. Add 2 tablespoons butter and 1 tablespoon oil to the reserved pan drippings. Sauté the onion in the butter mixture for 3 minutes or until tender. Stir in the bell pepper and garlic.

Cook for 3 to 5 minutes or until the bell pepper is tender-crisp, stirring frequently. Add the tomato, Worcestershire sauce and lemon juice and mix well. Return the chicken and shrimp to the skillet and mix well. Simmer for 5 minutes or until heated through, stirring occasionally. Spoon over the pasta on a serving platter.

Serves 6 to 8
Pearlie Miller, East Berry Branch

Greek Chicken Avgolemono

CHICKEN
1/2 cup olive oil
1/2 cup red wine
Juice of 2 small lemons
2 garlic cloves, minced
1/2 teaspoon oregano
Salt and pepper to taste
6 chicken breasts, skinned

AVGOLEMONO SAUCE
1/4 cup lemon juice
2 teaspoons cornstarch
4 eggs, beaten
2 cups chicken broth

For the chicken, whisk the olive oil, wine, lemon juice, garlic, oregano, salt and pepper in a shallow dish. Add the chicken and turn to coat. Marinate, covered, in the refrigerator for 8 to 10 hours, turning occasionally; drain. Arrange the chicken in a baking pan. Bake at 350 degrees for 45 minutes.

For the sauce, whisk the lemon juice, cornstarch and eggs in a bowl until blended. Heat the broth in a saucepan just to the boiling point. Add 1/2 cup of the hot broth to the egg mixture and mix well. Add the egg mixture to the hot broth, whisking constantly until blended. Bring to a boil over medium heat, stirring frequently. Boil for 1 minute or until thickened, stirring frequently. Arrange the chicken on a serving platter. Drizzle with the sauce.

Serves 6
Roberta Schenewerk, Central Library

Lemon Chicken

1 lemon, thickly sliced
6 chicken breasts
1/4 cup (1/2 stick) butter or margarine, melted
1/4 cup lemon juice
1 tablespoon chopped fresh parsley
1 teaspoon lemon pepper seasoning
1 (4-ounce) can sliced mushrooms, drained

Arrange the lemon slices in a single layer in a 9×13-inch baking dish. Top with the chicken. Drizzle with a mixture of the butter and lemon juice. Sprinkle with the parsley and lemon pepper seasoning.

Bake at 375 degrees for 30 minutes. Spoon the mushrooms around the chicken. Bake for 10 minutes longer or until the chicken is cooked through.

Serves 6
Pearlie Miller, East Berry Branch

Marsala Chicken

Jim Barnes is one of those cooks who likes to create his own dishes as he goes, throwing in a little of this and a pinch of that until the taste is just right. Most of the time this works very well. His Marsala Chicken recipe is one of his most delicious creations.

4 chicken breasts
2 tablespoons olive oil
½ large onion, sliced
1 (16-ounce) can chopped tomatoes
4 garlic cloves, crushed, chopped
1 bay leaf

1 teaspoon basil
¼ teaspoon salt
¼ teaspoon pepper
1 green bell pepper, sliced
½ cup marsala
1 tablespoon sugar

Brown the chicken on both sides in the olive oil in a skillet. Remove the chicken to a platter using a slotted spoon, reserving the pan drippings. Sauté the onion in the reserved pan drippings. Stir in the undrained tomatoes, garlic, bay leaf, basil, salt and pepper. Return the chicken to the skillet. Add the bell pepper, wine and sugar and mix well. Simmer, covered, over low heat until the chicken is cooked through, stirring occasionally. Discard the bay leaf.

Serves 4
Connie Barnes, Watauga Public Library

Slow-Cooker Chicken

1 jar dried beef
4 boneless skinless chicken breasts
4 slices bacon
¼ cup sour cream
1 tablespoon flour

1 (10-ounce) can cream of mushroom
  soup
⅓ cup water
Pepper to taste
Hot cooked noodles

Grease the side and bottom of a slow cooker lightly. Arrange the dried beef over the bottom and up the side of the slow cooker. Wrap each chicken breast with 1 slice of bacon and secure with a wooden pick. Place the chicken over the dried beef. Combine the sour cream and flour in a bowl and mix well. Stir in the soup, water and pepper. Spoon the sour cream mixture over the chicken. Cook on Low for 8 hours or on High for 5 hours. Serve over hot cooked noodles.

Serves 4
Lynne Harmon, Central Library

Sunburst Stir-Fry Chicken

1 boneless skinless chicken breast, cut into chunks
2 teaspoons vegetable oil
2 teaspoons ginger
1 teaspoon garlic powder
1 cup drained pineapple tidbits
2 medium carrots, sliced
1 green bell pepper, chopped
4 ounces thin spaghetti, cooked, drained
1/3 cup pineapple juice
1/3 cup soy sauce
1 tablespoon cornstarch
1 tablespoon vegetable oil
3 green onions, thinly sliced

Stir-fry the chicken in a mixture of 2 teaspoons oil, ginger and garlic powder in a skillet for 2 minutes. Add the pineapple, carrots and bell pepper. Steam, covered, for 2 to 3 minutes, stirring occasionally. Stir in the spaghetti. Combine the pineapple juice, soy sauce, cornstarch and 1 tablespoon oil in a bowl and mix well. Add to the chicken mixture and mix well. Stir in the green onions. Cook just until heated through, stirring frequently.

Serves 4
Lisa Harper Wood, Keller Public Library

Pressure-Cooker Barbecued Chicken

2 to 3 tablespoons vegetable oil
3 to 4 pounds chicken pieces, skinned
2 cups barbecue sauce
1 1/2 cups chopped onions
1 large green bell pepper, chopped

Heat 1 tablespoon of the oil in the pressure cooker. Brown the chicken on both sides in batches in the hot oil, adding the remaining oil as needed. Remove the chicken with a slotted spoon to a platter. Drain the pan drippings if desired.

Combine the barbecue sauce, onions and bell pepper in the pressure cooker and stir well to dislodge any browned bits. Add the chicken and any juices that have collected on the platter to the barbecue sauce mixture and stir until the chicken is well coated. Lock the lid in place. Bring to high pressure over high heat. Adjust the heat to maintain the high pressure. Cook for 9 minutes. Reduce the pressure with a quick release method using manufacturer's directions. Remove the lid, tilting it away from you to allow any excess steam to release. Arrange the chicken on a platter. Drizzle with the sauce.

Serves 4 to 6
Renée Cordray, Ridglea Branch

Sunday Chicken Legs

Super simple to prepare, the good flavor of this oven-fried, crisp-crusted chicken comes from the whole wheat flour coating.

½ cup whole wheat flour
1 teaspoon salt
1 teaspoon salad herbs (optional)
½ teaspoon seasoned salt

8 to 12 chicken legs or thighs, skinned
2 eggs, beaten
3 tablespoons margarine, melted
1 tablespoon teriyaki sauce

Combine the whole wheat flour, salt, salad herbs and seasoned salt in a shallow dish and mix well. Coat the chicken with the flour mixture and dip in the eggs. Coat the chicken with the remaining flour mixture again.

Arrange the chicken in a single layer in a buttered baking dish. Drizzle with the margarine. Bake at 450 degrees for 10 minutes. Reduce the oven temperature to 350 degrees. Bake for 25 minutes. Drizzle with the teriyaki sauce. Bake for 5 to 10 minutes longer or until the chicken is cooked through.

Serves 4 to 6
Corina Escamilla, Wedgwood Branch

Polynesian Wings

Chicken wings
2 large bottles soy sauce

6 or 7 bay leaves
¼ to ⅓ cup peppercorns

Separate each chicken wing into 2 pieces, discarding the tip. Place in a Dutch oven. Pour in enough soy sauce to cover the wings. Stir in the bay leaves and peppercorns.

Cook until the wings are tender, stirring occasionally. Discard the bay leaves and peppercorns. Spoon the chicken and sauce over hot cooked rice. May substitute ½ cup water for ½ cup of the soy sauce to decrease the sodium.

Makes a variable amount
Irene Roa, Wedgwood Branch

Soy sauce
A dark, salty sauce made by fermenting boiled soybeans and roasted wheat or barley.

Cheesy Chicken

A friend gave this recipe to me over twenty years ago. My children, who had a hard time agreeing on anything, all loved this dish.

Chopped onion to taste
1 can picante vegetable juice cocktail
2 (10-ounce) cans Cheddar cheese or
   Fiesta nacho soup, or 1 of each

1 pound cooked chicken, shredded
Tortilla chips

Sauté the onion in a nonstick skillet until tender. Stir in the vegetable juice cocktail. Cook until reduced by ½, stirring frequently. Add the soup and mix well. Stir in the chicken. Cook just until heated through, stirring frequently.

    Spoon the chicken mixture over tortilla chips on a platter. Garnish with chopped onions, chopped tomatoes, shredded lettuce, chile peppers, sour cream and/or guacamole.

Serves 4 to 6
Edith Beightol, Floater

Green Enchilada Casserole

1 (10-ounce) can cream of chicken
   soup
1 (10-ounce) can cream of mushroom
   soup
1 (5-ounce) can evaporated milk
2½ to 3 cups chopped cooked chicken

8 to 10 corn tortillas, torn
4 ounces (about) shredded cheese
1 (4-ounce) can chopped green chiles,
   drained
½ onion, chopped

Combine the soups and evaporated milk in a saucepan and mix well. Cook until heated through, stirring frequently. Stir in the chicken, tortillas, cheese, green chiles and onion.

    Spoon the chicken mixture into a baking dish. Bake at 350 degrees for 45 to 60 minutes or until brown and bubbly.

Serves 6
Dorothy Douglas, Haltom City Public Library

Chicken Tetrazzini

8 ounces spaghetti, broken
Salt to taste
1 tablespoon butter or margarine
1 onion, chopped
1 cup sliced mushrooms
1 garlic clove, finely chopped
2 tablespoons butter or margarine
1/4 cup flour

2 1/2 cups milk
Cayenne pepper to taste
1 (8-ounce) can water chestnuts,
   drained, sliced
1 cup chopped cooked chicken
2 tablespoons dry sherry
1/2 cup grated Parmesan cheese
Paprika to taste

Cook the spaghetti in boiling salted water in a saucepan for 10 minutes or until al dente; drain. Heat 1 tablespoon butter in a skillet over medium-low heat until melted. Add the onion, mushrooms and garlic and mix well. Cook for 3 minutes or until the onion is tender, stirring constantly. Remove the onion mixture to a bowl.

Heat 2 tablespoons butter in the skillet until melted. Whisk in the flour until blended. Cook for 2 to 3 minutes, stirring constantly; do not brown. Whisk in the milk, salt and cayenne pepper. Cook until slightly thickened, stirring constantly. Add the onion mixture, water chestnuts, chicken and sherry and mix well.

Layer the spaghetti, chicken mixture, cheese and paprika alternately in a greased 2-quart baking dish until all of the ingredients are used. Bake at 400 degrees for 30 minutes.

Serves 4 to 6
Pearlie Miller, East Berry Branch

Scalloped Chicken

3 1/2 cups chopped cooked chicken
1 cup finely chopped cooked carrots
1 cup peas
1/2 cup chopped potato
1/2 cup (1 stick) butter, softened

1 (10-ounce) can cream of mushroom
   soup
2 cups chicken broth
1/2 cup flour

Combine the chicken, carrots, peas, potato, butter and soup in a bowl and mix gently. Whisk the broth and flour in a bowl until smooth. Add the broth mixture to the chicken mixture and mix well. Spoon into a 9×13-inch baking dish. Bake at 325 degrees for 1 hour.

Serves 6
Linda Waggener, Floater

Burrito Casserole

4 or 5 burritos (any flavor)
1 (10-ounce) can cream of chicken
  soup
½ (4-ounce) can chopped green
  chiles, drained

Chopped onion to taste
Chopped green bell pepper to taste
Shredded Cheddar cheese to taste

Arrange the burritos in a single layer in a baking pan. Combine the soup, green chiles, onion and bell pepper in a bowl and mix well. Spoon the soup mixture over the burritos. Sprinkle with the cheese. Bake, covered with foil, at 350 degrees for 30 to 40 minutes or until bubbly.

Serves 4 or 5
Betty Howe, Keller Public Library

Salmon Loaf

This recipe is dedicated in memory of my mother, Janice Richardson. The Salmon Loaf was a favorite of my dad.

1 (16-ounce) can pink salmon
1½ cups bread crumbs
⅔ cup chopped celery
½ cup evaporated milk
2 eggs, beaten

1 tablespoon lemon juice
1 teaspoon salt
½ teaspoon baking powder
⅛ teaspoon cayenne pepper

Drain the salmon, reserving the liquid. Discard the skin and bones. Flake the salmon in a bowl. Combine the reserved liquid with enough water to measure ½ cup. Add to the salmon. Stir in the bread crumbs, celery, evaporated milk, eggs, lemon juice, salt, baking powder and cayenne pepper.

Shape the salmon mixture into a loaf in a greased glass loaf pan. Bake at 350 degrees for 30 to 40 minutes or until brown and firm. May shape the salmon mixture into patties and sauté in a skillet until light brown on both sides.

Serves 6
Karen Brown, Central Library

Salmon Rice Casserole

Salmon is an excellent source of calcium.

2 cups cooked rice
1 cup thinly sliced celery
¼ cup chopped fresh parsley, or 2
    tablespoons parsley flakes
¼ cup sliced green or black olives
½ cup mayonnaise
2 tablespoons French dressing

2 tablespoons lemon juice
1 (16-ounce) can salmon, drained,
    bones and skin removed
½ cup dry bread crumbs
2 tablespoons butter or margarine,
    melted

Combine the rice, celery, parsley and olives in a bowl and mix well. Stir in the mayonnaise, French dressing and lemon juice. Add the salmon and mix gently. Spoon the salmon mixture into a buttered 6-cup baking dish.

    Combine the bread crumbs and butter in a bowl and mix well. Sprinkle the bread crumb mixture over the top. Bake at 400 degrees for 25 to 30 minutes or until heated through. May freeze, covered, for future use.

Serves 4 to 6
Marion Edwards, Riverside Branch

Shrimp Spaghetti

¼ cup (½ stick) butter
¾ cup chopped green bell pepper
1 small onion, chopped
1 garlic clove, minced
¼ cup flour
2½ cups milk

1 (10-ounce) can tomato soup, heated
8 ounces sharp Cheddar cheese, cubed
8 to 16 ounces cooked shrimp,
    chopped or cut into halves
8 ounces spaghetti, cooked, drained

Heat the butter in a saucepan until melted. Add the bell pepper, onion and garlic and mix well. Simmer until the bell pepper and onion are tender, stirring frequently. Stir in the flour. Cook until bubbly, stirring constantly. Add the milk and mix well.

    Cook until thickened, stirring constantly. Stir in the hot condensed soup and cheese. Cook until the cheese melts, stirring constantly. Remove from heat. Stir in the shrimp. Spoon the shrimp mixture over the spaghetti on a serving platter.

Serves 4
Anne Noyes, Richland Hills Public Library

Chiles Rellenos

2 (7-ounce) cans whole green chiles,
  drained
1½ pounds Monterey Jack cheese,
  shredded
½ cup milk

4 eggs, lightly beaten
1 teaspoon salt
½ teaspoon dry mustard
¼ teaspoon pepper

Layer the green chiles and cheese ½ at a time in a lightly greased 7×11-inch baking dish. Whisk the milk, eggs, salt, dry mustard and pepper in a bowl until blended. Pour the milk mixture over the prepared layers. Bake at 350 degrees for 30 to 50 minutes or until brown and set. Cut into squares.

Serves 6 to 8
Betty Patterson, Richland Hills Public Library

Chile Relleno Casserole

My husband, Bob, grows Anaheim chiles in his garden every year. Fresh roasted green chiles are preferred, but canned green chiles may be substituted for the fresh.

20 whole green chiles, roasted
16 ounces Cheddar cheese, shredded
8 ounces Monterey Jack cheese,
  shredded

1½ cups milk
4 eggs
2 tablespoons flour

Line a 9×13-inch baking dish with half the green chiles. Sprinkle with the Cheddar cheese and Monterey Jack cheese. Top with the remaining green chiles. Whisk the milk, eggs and flour in a bowl until blended. Pour over the prepared layers. Bake at 350 degrees for 45 minutes or until a knife inserted in the center comes out clean.

To roast green chiles, make a 2-inch slit in each chile. It is best to wear gloves when handling fresh chiles. Arrange the chiles in a single layer on a broiler rack. Broil on the top oven rack until the skins are blackened, turning once. Remove to a sealable plastic bag immediately and seal tightly. Let stand for 15 minutes. Remove the stems, skin and seeds under cold running water. Use immediately or chill or freeze for future use. Thaw frozen green chiles in the refrigerator or under cold running water.

Serves 10
Marion Edwards, Riverside Branch

South-of-the-Border Pizza

1 (12-inch) prepared pizza crust
1 cup rinsed drained cooked kidney
    beans
1 cup frozen corn, thawed
1 tomato, chopped

¼ cup finely chopped fresh cilantro
1 jalapeño chile, finely chopped
¼ cup shredded reduced-fat Monterey
    Jack cheese
Green bell pepper strips (optional)

Place the pizza crust on an ungreased pizza pan or baking sheet. Arrange the beans, corn, tomato, cilantro and jalapeño chile over the crust. Sprinkle with the cheese.

    Bake at 450 degrees for 8 to 10 minutes or until light brown and bubbly. Garnish with bell pepper strips.

Serves 4
Hilda Olson, Central Library

Tofu and Brown Rice Casserole

This is one of my favorite casseroles. Vary the flavor by using different varieties of cheese and flavors of seasoned salt. Additional onions will also intensify the flavor.

1½ onions, thinly sliced
2 teaspoons vegetable oil, or 1½
    tablespoons butter or margarine
12 ounces tofu, pressed, cut into
    ½-inch cubes
1 cup cooked brown rice

1 teaspoon seasoned salt
⅛ teaspoon pepper
½ cup milk
½ cup shredded cheese
¼ cup bread crumbs

Sauté the onions in the oil in a skillet until light brown. Add the tofu and brown rice and mix well. Sauté for 2 minutes. Stir in the seasoned salt and pepper.

    Spoon the tofu mixture into a 6-cup baking dish sprayed with nonstick cooking spray. Pour the milk over the top. Sprinkle with the cheese and bread crumbs. Bake at 350 degrees for 15 to 20 minutes or until brown and bubbly.

Serves 4 to 6
Marion Edwards, Riverside Branch

VEGETABLES & SIDE DISHES

veg·e·ta·ble (vĕj′tə·bəl) *n.*

A edible plant whose seeds, roots, stems,
or leaves are used as food.

Shown above: Fort Worth Public Library, Book Stacks, 1939-1978

Cuban Black Beans

1 pound dried black beans
1 large onion, chopped
1 green bell pepper, chopped
1 (4-ounce) jar diced pimentos, drained
6 garlic cloves, minced
1/4 cup olive oil
5 cups water
1 (12-ounce) can tomato paste
1 tablespoon vinegar
2 teaspoons salt
1 teaspoon sugar
1 teaspoon pepper
Hot cooked rice
Shredded Cheddar cheese
Chopped tomatoes
Chopped green onions

Sort and rinse the beans. Combine the beans with enough water to cover by 2 inches in a bowl. Let stand for 8 hours; drain.

Sauté the onion, bell pepper, pimentos and garlic in the olive oil in a skillet until the vegetables are tender. Combine the beans, onion mixture, 5 cups water, tomato paste, vinegar, salt, sugar and pepper in a large saucepan or Dutch oven and mix well. Bring to a boil; reduce heat.

Simmer, covered, for 1½ hours or until the beans are tender, stirring occasionally. Spoon over hot cooked rice in individual bowls. Garnish with cheese, tomatoes and green onions.

Serves 8
Hilda Olson, Central Library

Pimento (Pih·MEN·toh)
The Spanish word for pepper, it is sweeter and more aromatic than the red bell pepper.

Classic Green Bean and Potato Casserole

My philosophy is that just about everything tastes better with cheese. I was out of cream of mushroom soup on one occasion and substituted cream of potato soup. Naturally, cream of potato soup tastes better with cheese, so my version of this classic dish was born. Enjoy!

1 (14-ounce) can green beans, drained
1 (10-ounce) can cream of potato soup
³⁄₄ cup milk
¹⁄₂ cup shredded Cheddar cheese
¹⁄₈ teaspoon pepper
1 (3-ounce) can French-fried onions

Combine the green beans, potato soup, milk, cheese and pepper in a bowl and mix well. Spoon into a 1¹⁄₂- or 2-quart baking dish sprayed with nonstick cooking spray.

Bake at 350 degrees for 20 to 25 minutes or until bubbly. Sprinkle with the onions. Bake for 5 minutes longer or until the onions are golden brown.

Serves 4 to 6
Mary Taggart Sikes, Central Library

Italian Green Beans

Two of my college professors at Northeastern Oklahoma State University were Italian. They invited all of their students to their home once a year for an authentic Italian meal. I have cooked green beans this way ever since.

1 (15-ounce) can cut green beans
2 teaspoons olive oil
1 teaspoon Italian herbs

Drain half the liquid from the beans. Place the beans and remaining liquid in a saucepan. Stir in the olive oil and Italian herbs; cover. Bring to a boil; reduce heat. Simmer for 10 to 15 minutes or until heated through, stirring occasionally.

Serves 2
Marion Edwards, Riverside Branch

Sesame Green Beans

12 ounces fresh green beans, trimmed
½ cup water
1 tablespoon margarine
1 tablespoon soy sauce
2 teaspoons sesame seeds, toasted

Combine the beans and water in a saucepan. Bring to a boil over
high heat; reduce heat to medium. Cook, covered, for 10 to 15 minutes
or until tender-crisp; drain. Add the margarine, soy sauce and
sesame seeds and toss to mix. Serve immediately.

Serves 3 or 4
Sylvia Autrey, Wedgwood Branch

Three-Bean Casserole

1 (16-ounce) can pork and beans
1 (16-ounce) can lima beans
1 (16-ounce) can kidney beans
4 ounces Colby cheese, cubed
6 slices bacon, crisp-cooked, chopped
1 medium onion, finely chopped
½ cup ketchup
½ cup packed brown sugar
2 tablespoons Worcestershire sauce

Combine the beans, cheese, bacon, onion, ketchup, brown sugar and
Worcestershire sauce in a bowl and mix well. Spoon the bean mixture
into a large baking dish. Bake at 350 degrees for 30 minutes, or
microwave for 15 minutes. Serve immediately.

Serves 8 to 10
Lisa Harper Wood, Keller Public Library

Cheesy Baked Broccoli and Cauliflower

Coming up with new ways to serve vegetables to a finicky crowd has always been a challenge. This recipe has become one of the most popular vegetable dishes I serve.

1 small head cauliflower
Salt to taste
Florets of 1 bunch broccoli
Pepper to taste

1 cup sour cream
2 cups shredded sharp Cheddar
   cheese

Remove the outer leaves of the cauliflower. Break into 1-inch florets. Blanch the cauliflower in boiling salted water in a saucepan for 5 minutes or just until tender; drain. Rinse with cold water to stop the cooking process. Repeat the process with the broccoli.

Layer the cauliflower, broccoli, salt, pepper, sour cream and cheese 1/2 at a time in a 9×13-inch baking dish. Bake at 350 degrees for 30 minutes or until bubbly.

Serves 6 to 8
Roberta Schenewerk, Central Library

Corn Casserole

2 (16-ounce) cans cream-style corn
2 cups shredded cheese
1 cup milk
1 (4-ounce) can chopped green chiles,
   drained

1/2 cup chopped onion
2 eggs, lightly beaten
1 cup yellow cornmeal
1/2 teaspoon garlic salt
1/2 teaspoon baking soda

Combine the corn, cheese, milk, green chiles, onion and eggs in a bowl and mix well. Combine the cornmeal, garlic salt and baking soda in a separate bowl and mix well. Stir the cornmeal mixture into the corn mixture.

Spoon the corn mixture into a greased 7×11-inch baking dish. Bake at 350 degrees for 50 minutes or until a knife inserted in the center comes out clean.

Serves 8
Renée Cordray, Ridglea Branch

Bourbon Corn Pudding

1 cup plus 2 tablespoons evaporated
   milk
3 eggs
3 cups cream-style corn
3 cups whole kernel corn
4½ tablespoons bourbon (optional)
3 tablespoons butter, melted

3 tablespoons brown sugar
¾ teaspoon nutmeg
⅜ teaspoon salt
⅜ teaspoon ground white pepper
3 tablespoons cornstarch
3 tablespoons water

Whisk the evaporated milk and eggs in a bowl until blended. Stir in the corn, bourbon, butter, brown sugar, nutmeg, salt and white pepper. Mix the cornstarch and water in a small bowl. Add the cornstarch mixture to the corn mixture and mix well.

    Spoon the corn mixture into a buttered baking dish. Bake at 350 degrees for 45 minutes or until light brown and a knife inserted in the center comes out clean. Serve immediately.

Serves 8 to 10
Hilda Olson, Central Library

Shoe Peg Surprise

3 (16-ounce) cans French-style green
   beans, drained
Salt and pepper to taste
2 (11-ounce) cans white Shoe Peg
   corn, drained
1 (10-ounce) can cream of celery soup

1 cup sour cream
2 cups shredded Cheddar cheese
1 to 1½ sleeves butter crackers,
   crushed
¾ cup (1½ sticks) butter, melted
1 cup chopped pecans or almonds

Spread the green beans evenly in a baking dish sprayed with nonstick cooking spray. Sprinkle with salt and pepper. Top with the corn and sprinkle with salt and pepper. Combine the soup and sour cream in a bowl and mix well. Spoon over the prepared layers. Sprinkle with the cheese. Top with the cracker crumbs and drizzle with the butter. Bake at 350 degrees for 30 to 40 minutes or until bubbly. Sprinkle with the pecans 5 to 10 minutes before the end of the baking process. Serve immediately.

    May prepare in advance and store, covered, in the refrigerator until ready to bake. Sprinkle with the cracker crumbs and drizzle with the butter just before baking.

Serves 6 to 8
Cheri Jewell, Central Library

Chile Eggplant Casserole

1/4 cup milk
2 eggs
1 large or 2 small eggplant, cut into
   1/2-inch slices
1 cup bread crumbs
2 tablespoons olive oil

1 (16-ounce) can stewed tomatoes
2 cups chopped green chiles
1 onion, chopped
16 ounces mozzarella cheese,
   shredded
1/4 cup grated Parmesan cheese

Whisk the milk and eggs in a bowl until blended. Dip the sliced eggplant in the egg mixture and coat with the bread crumbs. Fry the eggplant in the olive oil in a skillet until golden brown on both sides; drain. Layer the eggplant, undrained tomatoes, green chiles, onion and mozzarella cheese 1/2 at a time in an ungreased 9×13-inch baking dish. Sprinkle with the Parmesan cheese. Bake, covered, at 350 degrees for 45 minutes; remove cover. Bake for 15 minutes longer.

Serves 4 to 6
Hilda Olson, Central Library

Ratatouille with Basil

2 unpeeled eggplant, cubed
Salt to taste
1 Bermuda onion, finely chopped
2/3 cup sunflower oil
1 red bell pepper, chopped
1 green bell pepper, chopped

8 ounces zucchini, chopped
8 ounces tomatoes, peeled, chopped
2 garlic cloves, crushed
Pepper to taste
3 tablespoons chopped fresh basil

Sprinkle the eggplant with salt and place in a colander. Let stand for 20 minutes. Pat dry with paper towels. Cook the onion in the sunflower oil in a skillet over medium-low heat for 6 minutes, stirring occasionally. Stir in the eggplant and bell peppers. Cook for 10 minutes, adding additional oil if needed and stirring occasionally. Add the zucchini and mix well.

Cook for 5 minutes, stirring occasionally. Stir in the tomatoes and garlic. Cook for 10 minutes or until the vegetables are soft and slightly mushy, stirring occasionally. Season with salt and pepper. Remove from heat. Stir in the basil. Let stand for 4 to 5 minutes before serving. Serve hot or cold.

Serves 4 to 6
Sarah Harris, Riverside Branch

Potato Casserole

1 (2-pound) package frozen hash
   brown potatoes
½ cup (1 stick) butter, melted
10 ounces Cheddar cheese, shredded
1 (10-ounce) can cream of chicken
   soup
1 cup sour cream
½ cup chopped onion
1 can bread crumbs, or crushed
   cornflakes
¼ cup (½ stick butter), melted
1 (3-ounce) jar bacon bits

Spread the potatoes in a baking dish. Heat in a 350-degree oven just until thawed and warm. Combine the warm potatoes and ½ cup butter in a bowl and mix gently to coat. Combine the cheese, soup, sour cream and onion in a bowl and mix well. Add to the potato mixture and mix gently.

    Spoon the potato mixture into a buttered 9×12-inch baking dish. Sprinkle with a mixture of the bread crumbs and ¼ cup butter. Top with the bacon bits. Bake at 350 degrees for 45 minutes.

Serves 6
Mary Taggart Sikes, Central Library

Armadillo Potatoes

This recipe started out with a totally different name. The first time I served these potatoes my dinner guests renamed them because they resembled armadillos curled up in a ball. Thus the name has stuck.

6 unpeeled potatoes
¼ cup (½ stick) margarine, melted
1 envelope garlic-herb soup mix
¼ teaspoon sage
¼ teaspoon rosemary
Freshly ground pepper to taste

Cut the potatoes crosswise ¾ way through into ⅛-inch slices. Place the potatoes cut side up in a greased baking pan. Combine the margarine, soup mix, sage and rosemary in a bowl and mix well. Brush the potatoes with the margarine mixture. Sprinkle liberally with pepper.

    Bake at 375 degrees for 1¼ hours or until golden brown and slightly crisp, brushing with the remaining margarine mixture once or twice during the baking process.

Serves 6
Roberta Schenewerk, Central Library

Cheddar Baked Potato Slices

4 to 6 small red potatoes, sliced
1 cup shredded Cheddar cheese
1 (10-ounce) can golden mushroom
   soup
1/2 teaspoon paprika
1/2 teaspoon pepper

Arrange the potatoes in overlapping rows or circles in a greased 2-quart round or oblong baking dish. Sprinkle with the cheese. Combine the soup, paprika and pepper in a bowl and mix well. Spoon the soup mixture over the prepared layers.

    Bake, covered with foil, at 400 degrees for 45 minutes; remove cover. Bake for 10 minutes longer or until the potatoes are tender.

Serves 6
Ellen Warthoe, Ridglea/Wedgwood Branches

Escalloped Potatoes

This was one of the staple Sunday side dishes my mother prepared during my childhood. She would place the potatoes in a cold oven and then turn on the oven just before leaving for Sunday school. By the time we returned from church, all she had to do was add the cheese.

6 potatoes, peeled, thinly sliced
Butter to taste
Salt to taste
1 cup shredded Cheddar cheese
1/4 to 1/2 cup milk

Layer the potatoes, butter, salt and cheese alternately in a buttered baking dish until all of the ingredients are used. Do not sprinkle the remaining cheese on the top at this point. Pour the milk over the prepared layers; cover with foil.

    Bake at 350 degrees for 30 minutes. Remove the foil and sprinkle with the reserved cheese. Bake for 30 minutes longer. May place the potatoes in a cold oven and bake at 300 degrees for 1 1/2 hours. Remove the foil and sprinkle with the reserved cheese. Bake for 30 minutes longer. May add chopped cooked ham, broccoli or peas. Substitute seasoned salt for the salt and any variety cheese for the Cheddar cheese if desired.

Serves 6
Marion Edwards, Riverside Branch

Mashed Potato Casserole

8 to 10 medium potatoes,
 cut into quarters
Salt and pepper to taste
8 ounces cream cheese, softened
2 eggs, lightly beaten
2 tablespoons flour

2 tablespoons minced fresh parsley
2 tablespoons minced fresh chives, or
 1 small onion, minced
1 (3-ounce) can French-fried onions,
 crushed

Combine the potatoes with enough water to cover in a saucepan. Bring to a boil.
Boil until tender; drain. Beat the potatoes in a mixing bowl until smooth. Season
with salt and pepper. Add the cream cheese. Beat until blended. Add the eggs,
flour, parsley and chives and mix well. Adjust the seasonings.
 Spoon the potato mixture into a buttered baking dish. Top with the onions.
Bake at 325 degrees for 30 minutes or until puffy and golden brown. May be prepared
several hours in advance and stored, covered, in the refrigerator. Sprinkle with the
onions just before baking.

Serves 8
Sylvia Autrey, Wedgwood Branch

Rosemary Hash Brown Potatoes

2 tablespoons olive oil
1 garlic clove, minced
2 teaspoons fresh snipped rosemary
1½ pounds unpeeled red potatoes,
 cut into ½-inch cubes

½ teaspoon salt
½ teaspoon pepper
Sprigs of rosemary (optional)
Tomato wedges (optional)

Heat the olive oil in a skillet over medium heat. Add the garlic and 2 teaspoons
rosemary and mix well. Cook for 2 minutes, stirring constantly. Add the potatoes,
salt and pepper and mix well.
 Cook for 5 minutes, stirring occasionally. Reduce the heat to medium-low. Cook
for 20 minutes longer or until the potatoes are golden brown and crisp, turning
occasionally. Spoon into a serving bowl. Top with sprigs of rosemary and tomato
wedges. Serve immediately.

Serves 4 to 6
Hilda Olson, Central Library

Sweet Potato Casserole

3 cups mashed cooked sweet potatoes
¾ cup (1½ sticks) margarine, melted
1 (12-ounce) can evaporated milk
1½ cups sugar
2 eggs, beaten

½ teaspoon nutmeg
½ teaspoon cinnamon
1 cup crushed cornflakes
½ cup packed brown sugar
½ cup chopped pecans

Combine the sweet potatoes, margarine, evaporated milk, sugar, eggs, nutmeg and cinnamon in a bowl and mix well; the mixture will be thin. Spoon into a 9×13-inch baking dish. Bake at 400 degrees for 15 minutes.

Combine the cornflakes, brown sugar and pecans in a bowl and mix well. Sprinkle over the baked layer. Bake for 15 minutes longer.

Serves 4
Clark Strickland, Ella Mae Shamblee Branch

Yellow Squash Casserole

2 pounds yellow squash, sliced
  (6 cups)
¼ cup chopped onion
Salt to taste
1 (10-ounce) can cream of chicken
  soup

1 cup sour cream
1 cup shredded carrots
1 (8-ounce) package herb-seasoned
  stuffing mix
½ cup (1 stick) margarine, melted

Combine the squash, onion and salt with enough water to cover in a saucepan. Bring to a boil. Boil for 5 minutes; drain. Combine the soup and sour cream in a bowl and mix well. Stir in the carrots. Fold in the squash mixture.

Combine the stuffing mix and margarine in a bowl and mix well. Spread half the stuffing mixture in a lightly buttered 7×12-inch baking dish. Spoon the squash mixture into the prepared baking dish. Sprinkle with the remaining stuffing mixture. Bake at 350 degrees for 25 to 30 minutes or until heated through.

Serves 6 to 8
Renée Cordray, Ridglea Branch

Nutmeg
A seed from the nutmeg tree, a tropical evergreen, native to the Spice Islands.

Squash and Onions

2 pounds yellow squash, thickly sliced
1/4 cup sugar
1/2 teaspoon salt
1/4 teaspoon pepper
1 medium onion, chopped
1 tablespoon bacon drippings

Steam the squash until tender; drain. Mash the squash in a bowl. Stir in the sugar, salt and pepper. Sauté the onion in the bacon drippings in a skillet until the onion turns yellow. Stir in the squash mixture. Cook over medium heat until thickened, stirring constantly.

Serves 8
Raydene Rankin, Southwest Regional Library

Squash Supreme

2 cups sliced yellow squash, cooked, drained
1 (10-ounce) can cream of chicken soup
1 cup sour cream
1 carrot, grated
1 small onion, chopped
Salt and pepper to taste
Herb-seasoned bread crumbs
Butter to taste

Mash the squash in a bowl. Stir in the soup, sour cream, carrot and onion. Season with salt and pepper. Sprinkle bread crumbs over the bottom of a shallow baking dish. Spoon the squash mixture over the bread crumbs. Top with additional bread crumbs. Dot generously with butter.

Bake at 350 degrees for 30 to 45 minutes or until bubbly and the top is brown.

Serves 6 to 8
Karen Brown, Central Library

Summer Squash Bake

3 cups sliced yellow squash
2 tablespoons water
½ cup finely chopped green bell
   pepper
½ cup finely chopped onion
½ cup chopped pecans

½ cup mayonnaise
⅓ cup shredded Cheddar cheese
½ teaspoon sugar
½ teaspoon salt
¼ teaspoon pepper
⅓ cup shredded Cheddar cheese

Combine the squash and water in a microwave-safe bowl. Microwave for 4 to 5 minutes or until tender-crisp; drain. Stir in the bell pepper, onion, pecans, mayonnaise, ⅓ cup cheese, sugar, salt and pepper.

Spoon the squash mixture into a greased baking dish. Bake, covered, at 350 degrees for 25 minutes; remove cover. Sprinkle with ⅓ cup cheese. Bake for 5 minutes longer.

Serves 6
Sylvia Autrey, Wedgwood Branch

Spaghetti Squash

1 (2-pound) spaghetti squash
2 cups water
2 tablespoons olive oil
2 tablespoons minced fresh basil

1 large garlic clove, minced
½ teaspoon salt
⅛ teaspoon crushed hot pepper flakes

Make a ½-inch deep slash through the exterior skin of the squash from stem to stem. Place the squash in a pressure cooker. Add the water and cover. Bring to high pressure. Reduce the heat to stabilize the pressure. Cook for 20 minutes. Let the pressure release naturally; drain.

Cut the squash into halves, following the original slash marks. Scoop out the seeds and spongy membrane and discard. Transfer the squash to a bowl and separate into strands using 2 forks. Stir in the olive oil, basil, garlic, salt and hot pepper flakes. Serve immediately.

Serves 4
Renée Cordray, Ridglea Branch

Stuffed Green Peppers

6 large green bell peppers
5 cups boiling water
1½ pounds lean ground beef
2 tablespoons chopped onion
1 cup cooked rice
1 cup tomato juice

½ teaspoon salt
⅛ teaspoon garlic powder
6 thick tomato slices
Salt, grated Parmesan cheese or
    chopped fresh parsley to taste

Cut a thin slice from the stem end of each bell pepper. Remove the seeds and membranes. Combine the bell peppers with the boiling water in a saucepan. Cook for 5 minutes; drain. Brown the ground beef with the onion in a skillet, stirring until the ground beef is crumbly and the onion is tender; drain. Stir in the rice, tomato juice, ½ teaspoon salt and garlic powder. Bring to a boil, stirring frequently. Remove from heat.

    Spoon ½ cup of the rice mixture into each bell pepper. Arrange the bell peppers upright in an ungreased baking dish. Bake, covered with foil, for 45 minutes. Remove the bell peppers to a serving platter. Top each bell pepper with 1 tomato slice. Sprinkle with salt to taste, Parmesan cheese or parsley.

Serves 6
Gerry Humphreys, Wedgwood Branch

Orzo Rice Pilaf

This combination of two recipes makes a satisfying and out-of-the ordinary side dish.

¼ cup (½ stick) butter or margarine
1 cup orzo
1 small onion, chopped
1 cup shredded carrots
1 teaspoon minced garlic

1 teaspoon chives
4 cups chicken broth
1 cup long grain rice
2 teaspoons Greek seasoned salt

Heat the butter in a 2-quart saucepan until melted. Stir in the orzo, onion and carrots. Cook until the orzo is light golden brown, stirring frequently. Add the garlic and chives and mix well. Cook for 1 minute, stirring constantly. Stir in the broth, rice and seasoned salt. Bring to a boil; reduce heat to low. Simmer, covered, until the liquid is absorbed and the orzo and rice are tender.

Serves 6
Roberta Schenewerk, Central Library

MeMaw's Mac and Cheese

This recipe makes the best mac and cheese I have ever had and has become a must whenever our families gather.

2 (16-ounce) packages large
  sea shell macaroni
Salt to taste

2 pounds Velveeta cheese, cubed
1 cup milk
6 tablespoons margarine

Cook the pasta using package directions in boiling salted water in a stockpot; drain, leaving a small amount of liquid in the pan. Add the cheese, milk and margarine immediately and mix well. Serve immediately.

Serves 12 to 15
Brenda Lanche, Riverside Branch

Pasta with Fresh Basil Pesto

Pasta al pesto is an all-time favorite dish, even for non-Italians. Makes a great summertime main entrée. Be sure to use fresh basil when available.

FRESH BASIL PESTO
2 cups fresh basil leaves
1/3 cup pine nuts
2 or 3 garlic cloves
1/2 cup grated Parmesan cheese
1/4 cup grated Romano cheese
1/2 cup olive oil

PASTA
16 ounces shaped curvy pasta
3 tablespoons olive oil
2 tablespoons pine nuts
1/4 cup grated Parmesan cheese

For the pesto, reserve several basil leaves for garnish. Combine the remaining basil, the pine nuts and garlic in a blender or food processor container. Process until of the desired consistency. Add the Parmesan cheese and Romano cheese. Process briefly. Add the olive oil. Process until blended.

Cook the pasta using package directions until al dente; drain. Toss the pasta with the olive oil in a bowl until coated. Let stand until room temperature. Add the pesto and toss to mix. Sprinkle with the pine nuts and Parmesan cheese. Garnish with the reserved basil. Serve at room temperature or as a cold side dish. May decrease the amounts of garlic and olive oil according to taste.

Serves 6 to 8
Ellen Warthoe, Ridglea/Wedgwood Branches

Chinese Fried Rice

4 cups cold water
2 cups long grain rice
1 tablespoon salt
¼ cup vegetable oil
1 pound beef, pork or chicken,
    cooked, chopped
8 ounces deveined peeled cooked
    shrimp, chopped (optional)

Chopped onion to taste
2 tablespoons soy sauce
Chopped bell pepper to taste
Chopped celery to taste
2 eggs, beaten

Combine the water, rice and salt in a saucepan; cover. Bring to a boil over high heat; reduce heat to low. Simmer for 14 minutes; do not stir. Remove cover and simmer for 5 minutes longer; do not stir. The grains should be separated and fluffy. Chill, covered, in the refrigerator.

Heat the oil in a skillet over medium-high heat. Stir in the beef, shrimp, onion, soy sauce and rice. Stir-fry until the rice is brown. Cook for 1 minute more, stirring constantly. Add the bell pepper and celery and drizzle with the eggs. Cook for 2 minutes, stirring constantly. Serve immediately.

Serves 6
Brenda Lanche, Riverside Branch

Curried Lentil Rice

½ cup dried lentils
½ cup chopped green bell pepper
½ cup chopped onion
1 teaspoon finely chopped garlic
1 tablespoon vegetable oil

½ cup rice
½ teaspoon salt
½ teaspoon curry powder
1 (14-ounce) can chicken broth
¼ cup water

Sort and rinse the lentils. Sauté the bell pepper, onion and garlic in the oil in a skillet until the vegetables are tender. Stir in the lentils, rice, salt and curry powder. Cook for 1 minute, stirring frequently. Add the broth and water and mix well.

Simmer, covered, for 20 minutes or until the lentils and rice are tender. Let stand, covered, for 5 minutes before serving.

Serves 6 to 8
Ellen Warthoe, Ridglea/Wedgwood Branches

BREADS & BRUNCH

brunch (brŭnch) *n*.

A late morning meal that serves both as breakfast and lunch.

Shown above: Carnegie Public Library, Main Lobby, 1901-1938

Quick Cheese Biscuit Bread

For over fifteen years my husband and I have been taking turns cooking Saturday night dinners with two other couples. This has become one of our favorite bread recipes over the years. It is a simple quick bread that looks impressive when served.

1/4 cup (1/2 stick) butter or margarine, melted
1/2 teaspoon Worcestershire sauce
1/2 teaspoon minced chives

1/4 teaspoon garlic salt
2 (10-count) cans biscuits
1 cup finely shredded Cheddar cheese

Combine the butter, Worcestershire sauce, chives and garlic salt in a bowl and mix well. Separate the biscuits. Dip each biscuit in the butter mixture and sprinkle with cheese. Arrange the biscuits overlapping in an upright position in a greased 8- or 9-inch round baking pan or a 5-inch ring mold. Bake at 400 degrees for 15 to 20 minutes or until light brown. Invert onto a round serving platter immediately.

Serves 8
Roberta Schenewerk, Central Library

Chipotle Corn Bread

Chipotles are smoked and dried jalapeño chiles. They are readily available in most supermarkets.

1 cup unbleached flour
1/4 cup coarse-ground yellow cornmeal, or masa harina
1 tablespoon sugar
1 1/2 teaspoons baking powder
1/2 teaspoon salt

1/4 cup buttermilk
2 eggs
1/3 cup corn oil
2 canned whole chipotle chiles in adobo
1 cup shredded Monterey Jack cheese

Heat a greased cast-iron skillet in a 400-degree oven. Combine the flour, cornmeal, sugar, baking powder and salt in a bowl and mix well. Process the buttermilk, eggs, corn oil and chipotle chiles in a food processor or blender until the chiles are finely chopped. Add the buttermilk mixture and cheese to the cornmeal mixture, mixing with a spoon or rubber spatula just until blended; do not overmix. Pour the batter into the hot skillet. Bake for 20 to 25 minutes or until golden brown around the edge and tests done. Let stand for 15 minutes before cutting into wedges.

Serves 6 to 8
Hilda Olson, Central Library

Aunt Pearl's Banana Nut Bread

Some recipes shine with the memory of certain people. This one reminds my family of Aunt Pearl's generous and kind nature.

2 cups baking mix
1 cup sugar
½ teaspoon nutmeg
½ teaspoon cinnamon

1 cup (or more) mashed bananas
2 eggs
2 tablespoons butter, melted
1 cup chopped walnuts

Combine the baking mix, sugar, nutmeg and cinnamon in a mixing bowl and mix well. Add the bananas, eggs and butter. Beat just until blended. Stir in the walnuts. Spoon the batter into a greased and floured 4×8-inch loaf pan. Bake at 350 degrees for 1 hour. Cool in pan for 10 minutes. Remove to a wire rack to cool completely.

Makes 1 loaf
Lynn Allen, Diamond Hill/Jarvis Branch

Chocolate Banana Bread

2 cups flour
¼ cup baking cocoa
1 teaspoon baking soda
1 teaspoon salt
1 cup sugar
½ cup (1 stick) margarine, softened

1 cup mashed bananas (about
 2 bananas)
¼ cup milk
2 eggs
1 teaspoon vanilla extract
¾ to 1 cup chopped pecans

Combine the flour, baking cocoa, baking soda and salt in a bowl and mix well. Combine the sugar and margarine in a mixing bowl. Beat until creamy, scraping the bowl occasionally. Add the bananas, milk, eggs and vanilla. Beat until blended. Add the flour mixture. Beat just until moistened. Fold in the pecans.

Spoon the batter into a greased 5×9-inch loaf pan. Bake at 350 degrees for 60 to 65 minutes or until a wooden pick inserted in the center comes out clean. Cool in pan for 10 minutes. Remove to a wire rack to cool completely.

Makes 1 loaf
Sylvia Autrey, Wedgwood Branch

Cranberry Nut Bread

*It's the addition of orange juice and orange zest that makes this
bread so good and moist.*

2 cups flour
1 cup sugar
1½ teaspoons baking powder
1 teaspoon salt
½ teaspoon baking soda
¾ cup orange juice
2 tablespoons shortening
1 tablespoon grated orange zest
1 egg, beaten
1½ cups fresh or frozen cranberries, coarsely chopped
½ cup chopped nuts

Combine the flour, sugar, baking powder, salt and baking soda in a
bowl and mix well. Stir in the orange juice, shortening, orange zest
and egg. Add the cranberries and nuts and mix well.

Spoon the batter into a greased 5×9-inch loaf pan. Bake at 350
degrees for 55 minutes or until a wooden pick inserted in the center
comes out clean. Cool in pan on a wire rack for 15 minutes. Remove
to rack to cool completely.

Makes 1 loaf
Eric Fry, Central Library

Apple Allspice Muffins

These muffins have a moist cake-like texture.

TOPPING
1/4 cup (1/2 stick) margarine, softened
1/3 cup flour
1/4 cup packed brown sugar
1/2 teaspoon allspice

MUFFINS
1 1/2 cups flour
2 teaspoons baking powder
1/2 teaspoon allspice
1/4 teaspoon salt
1/2 cup packed brown sugar
1/4 cup (1/2 stick) margarine, softened
1 egg
3/4 cup milk
1 cup finely chopped apple
1/2 cup chopped pecans

For the topping, combine the margarine, flour, brown sugar and allspice in a bowl and mix well.

For the muffins, combine the flour, baking powder, allspice and salt in a bowl and mix well. Beat the brown sugar and margarine in a mixing bowl until creamy. Add the egg. Beat until blended. Add the flour mixture alternately with the milk, mixing just until blended after each addition. Fold in the apple and pecans. Fill greased muffins cups 2/3 full. Sprinkle with the topping. Bake at 400 degrees for 20 minutes. Serve warm.

Makes 1 dozen muffins
Corina Escamilla, Wedgwood Branch

Banana Pecan Muffins

Do not overmix or tops will be peaked instead of rounded.

2 cups flour
1 teaspoon salt
1 teaspoon baking powder
½ teaspoon baking soda
1 cup sugar
½ cup (1 stick) margarine, softened
2 large ripe bananas, mashed
2 eggs, lightly beaten
⅓ cup buttermilk
½ cup chopped pecans
1 teaspoon vanilla extract

Combine the flour, salt, baking powder and baking soda in a bowl and mix well. Combine the sugar and margarine in a mixing bowl. Beat until creamy. Add the bananas and eggs. Beat until light and fluffy. Add the flour mixture to the creamed mixture alternately with the buttermilk, mixing just until moistened after each addition. Fold in the pecans and vanilla.

Fill each greased muffin cup with ½ cup of the batter. Bake at 400 degrees for 15 to 18 minutes or until golden brown. Serve hot. Leftovers may be reheated.

Makes 1 dozen muffins
Corina Escamilla, Wedgwood Branch

Buttermilk
In the past, was the liquid which remained after the cream was churned into butter; has a slightly thickened texture and tangy flavor.

Prune Spice Muffins

Great for breakfast or brunch.

¾ cup whole wheat flour
1 cup all-purpose flour
2 tablespoons sugar
2 teaspoons baking powder
1 teaspoon cinnamon
¼ teaspoon salt
¼ cup (½ stick) margarine
1 cup milk
1 egg, lightly beaten
¾ cup pitted cooked prunes, chopped
¼ cup chopped pecans

Combine the whole wheat flour, all-purpose flour, sugar, baking powder, cinnamon and salt in a bowl and mix well. Cut in the margarine until crumbly. Add the milk and egg and stir just until moistened. Fold in the prunes and pecans.

Fill greased muffin cups ¾ full. Bake at 425 degrees for 15 to 20 minutes. Serve immediately.

May substitute 2 cups all-purpose flour for the mixture of ¾ cup whole wheat flour and 1 cup all-purpose flour.

Makes 1 dozen muffins
Corina Escamilla, Wedgwood Branch

East Texas Butter Rolls

My sister-in-law is from east Texas. She kept asking me about butter rolls and I thought she was referring to yeast breads. I finally acquired this recipe from a friend's grandmother who resides in east Texas. This recipe was developed when fruit and pie fillings were scarce. I now have requests to make these rolls frequently.

1 recipe pie pastry
1 cup (2 sticks) butter or margarine, softened
1½ cups sugar
2 tablespoons cinnamon
1 tablespoon nutmeg
1 (12-ounce) can evaporated milk
1 evaporated milk can of water

Divide the pastry into 12 equal portions. Roll each portion into a 6-inch circle on a lightly floured surface. Spread each pastry circle with some of the butter. Mix the sugar, cinnamon and nutmeg in a bowl. Sprinkle some over each pastry circle. Roll to enclose the filling.

Arrange the rolls seam side down in a 9×13-inch baking dish. Pour the evaporated milk over the rolls. Pour the water over the rolls. Sprinkle with the remaining sugar mixture and dot with the remaining butter. Bake at 350 degrees until the rolls are light brown and the sauce is thickened. Serve warm. May top the rolls with desired flavor of pie filling.

Makes 1 dozen rolls
Barbara M. Smith, Central Library (retired)

Sandwich Bread

Some of our favorite sandwich fillings are smoked turkey, ham, roast beef, peppered cheese, American cheese, sliced tomatoes, onions, black olives and lettuce with ranch dressing.

2 packages hot roll mix
Melted butter

Prepare the hot roll mix using package directions. Shape the dough into 8 loaves and place on baking sheets. Bake using package directions until almost done. Brush the tops of the loaves with butter. Bake until the loaves test done. Remove to a wire rack to cool. Slice as desired for sandwiches.

Makes 8 loaves
Brenda McCrary, Richland Hills Public Library

Brunch Casserole

1 pound mild sausage
2 cups milk
6 eggs
1 teaspoon salt
1 teaspoon dry mustard
2 slices white bread, cubed
1 cup shredded mild cheese

Brown the sausage in a skillet, stirring until crumbly; drain. Whisk the milk, eggs, salt and dry mustard in a bowl until blended. Add the sausage, bread and cheese and mix gently. Pour the sausage mixture into a buttered 9×13-inch baking dish. Chill, covered, for 8 to 10 hours.

Place the baking dish in a cold oven. Bake at 350 degrees for 45 minutes. Serve immediately.

Serves 6 to 8
Marion Edwards, Riverside Branch

Country Grits and Sausage Casserole

1 pound hot pork bulk sausage
4 cups water
1¼ cups quick-cooking grits
4 cups shredded sharp Cheddar cheese
1 cup milk
1 teaspoon salt
½ teaspoon thyme
½ teaspoon garlic powder
4 eggs, beaten
Shredded sharp Cheddar cheese to taste

Brown the sausage in a skillet, stirring until crumbly; drain. Bring the water to a boil in a saucepan. Stir in the grits. Return to a boil; reduce heat. Simmer, covered, for 5 minutes, stirring occasionally. Remove from heat. Add 4 cups cheese, milk, salt, thyme and garlic powder and stir until the cheese melts. Add the sausage and eggs and mix well.

Spoon the grits mixture into a greased 9×13-inch baking pan. Sprinkle with cheese. Bake at 350 degrees for 1 hour or until golden brown. Let stand for 5 minutes before serving. May be prepared 1 day in advance and stored, covered, in the refrigerator. Let stand, covered, at room temperature for 30 minutes before baking. Remove the cover before baking.

Serves 10
Roberta Schenewerk, Central Library

Grits
Any coarsely ground grain such as corn, oats or rice, but most commonly refers to "hominy grits."

Sausage Grits

1 pound bulk sausage
3 cups hot cooked grits
2½ cups shredded Cheddar cheese
3 tablespoons butter or margarine
1½ cups milk
3 eggs
Pimento strips (optional)
Sprigs of parsley (optional)

Brown the sausage in a skillet, stirring until crumbly; drain. Spread the sausage over the bottom of a baking dish. Combine the hot grits, cheese and butter in a bowl and stir until the cheese and butter melt. Whisk the milk and eggs in a bowl until blended. Add to the grits mixture and mix well.

Spoon the grits mixture over the sausage. Bake at 350 degrees for 1 hour. Top with pimento strips and parsley. May be prepared 1 day in advance and stored, covered, in the refrigerator. Bake just before serving.

Serves 15
Marion Edwards, Riverside Branch

Morning Glories

The Support Services staff of the library has quarterly breakfast birthday parties. We have breakfast because the couriers have to get on the road early and do not return until late in the day. As a result, I am always searching for new and innovative breakfast recipes. This is one of the more unique ones. These "cookies" make a good one-handed breakfast for people on the go. Don't let the ingredients fool you. These are not sweet.

2 cups quick-cooking oats
1 cup cornmeal
1 cup flour
3/4 teaspoon baking soda
1/2 teaspoon salt
3/4 cup (1 1/2 sticks) butter or margarine, softened
3/4 cup packed brown sugar
2 eggs
1 tablespoon prepared mustard
1 1/2 cups chopped cooked link sausage
1 cup shredded Cheddar cheese

Combine the oats, cornmeal, flour, baking soda and salt in a bowl and mix well. Combine the butter and brown sugar in a mixing bowl. Beat until light and fluffy, scarping the bowl occasionally. Add the eggs and prepared mustard. Beat until blended. Add the oats mixture and beat until mixed. Stir in the sausage and cheese.

Drop the dough by scant 1/4 cupfuls 3 inches apart onto a greased baking sheet. Bake at 350 degrees for 15 to 17 minutes or until light brown. Cool on baking sheet for 1 minute. Remove to a wire rack. Serve warm.

Reheat in a microwave for 15 to 30 seconds or in a 350-degree oven for 3 minutes. Store in an airtight container in the refrigerator.

Makes 1 1/2 dozen
Roberta Schenewerk, Central Library

Potato Omelet with Pepperoni

1/2 cup vegetable oil
6 medium potatoes, thinly sliced
1 large onion, minced
8 eggs, beaten
1 1/2 cups chopped pepperoni
1 teaspoon salt
1/4 teaspoon pepper

Heat the oil in a large skillet over medium heat. Add the potatoes and fry until cooked through. Remove the potatoes to paper towels to drain using a slotted spoon, reserving the pan drippings. Sauté the onion in the reserved pan drippings until tender; drain. Combine the potatoes and onion in a bowl and mix gently. Add the eggs, pepperoni, salt and pepper and mix well.

Pour the egg mixture into a skillet, tilting the skillet to ensure even coverage. Cook over medium heat for 15 minutes. Slide the half-cooked omelet onto a plate and turn it over into the skillet. Cook until firm. Slice as desired. Serve immediately. May substitute mushrooms or chorizo for the pepperoni.

Serves 8 to 10
Rina Lutts, Haltom City Public Library

Sheet Quiche

PASTRY
1 cup shortening, or ½ cup margarine
    and ½ cup shortening
3¼ cups flour
1 teaspoon salt
Ice water

ASSEMBLY
1 cup shredded Gruyère or Swiss
    cheese

SPINACH FILLING
2 (10-ounce) packages frozen spinach,
    thawed, drained
6 green onions, chopped
6 tablespoons butter or margarine
3 cups half-and-half or evaporated
    milk
9 eggs
Salt and pepper to taste

For the pastry, cut the shortening into the flour in a bowl until crumbly or process in a food processor. Stir in the salt. Add ice water 1 tablespoon at a time, mixing with a fork until the mixture forms an easily handled ball. Chill, wrapped in plastic wrap, for 1 hour. Roll the pastry into a large rectangle on a lightly floured surface. Press over the bottom and up the sides of a 10×15-inch baking sheet with sides. Chill for 30 minutes. If dough is very soft, cover with foil. Bake at 350 degrees for 15 minutes; remove foil. Bake for 12 minutes longer.

For the filling, press the excess moisture from spinach. Sauté the green onions in the butter in a skillet until tender. Stir in the spinach. Sauté for 2 minutes. Remove from heat. Whisk the half-and-half and eggs in a bowl until blended. Add to the spinach mixture and mix well. Season with salt and pepper.

To assemble, sprinkle the cheese over the pastry. Pour the spinach filling over the cheese. Bake at 350 degrees until puffed and set. Cut as desired.

For variety, omit one 10-ounce package spinach, add 2 cups crumbled crisp-cooked bacon or chopped ham and substitute Cheddar cheese for the Gruyère cheese. Or, substitute 2 cups chopped zucchini for the spinach, add cups browned sausage and your choice of cheese. Or, omit the spinach and add 2 cups shredded cheese of your choice and chopped red bell pepper for color.

Serves 8 to 10
Keith Miller, Central Library

Gruyère (groo·YEHR)
Cheese made from cow's milk and named for the Gruyère Valley in Switzerland. It has a rich, sweet nutty flavor.

Brunch Tortillas

1 small package frozen hash brown
  potatoes
1 pound sausage
1 medium green bell pepper, finely
  chopped
Finely chopped onion to taste

2 to 3 tablespoons butter
10 eggs, beaten
Salt and pepper to taste
8 to 12 (10-inch) flour tortillas,
  heated
Shredded cheese

Cook the potatoes using package directions. Cover to keep warm. Brown the
sausage in a skillet, stirring until crumbly; drain. Sauté the bell pepper and onion
in the butter until tender. Add the eggs, salt and pepper and mix well. Cook until
soft scrambled. Stir in the sausage. Remove from heat.

Spoon about 2 tablespoons of the sausage mixture onto each tortilla. Top with
about 1 tablespoon of the potatoes and sprinkle with cheese. Fold the ends in and
roll to enclose the filling. Wrap each tortilla in foil. Place on a baking sheet.

Bake at 325 degrees for 20 to 25 minutes or until heated through. Serve with
picante sauce. May be prepared in advance and frozen for future use. Thaw in the
refrigerator for 30 minutes before baking.

Serves 8 to 12
Irene Clark, great aunt of Clark Strickland, Ella Mae Shamblee Branch

Megas Corn Tortillas and Eggs

*My two children and I have enjoyed this both as a morning and evening meal.
Their paternal Grandfather Balderas introduced us to this dish. He is on our minds
every time I prepare this recipe. Now I will share with you and your family.*

4 to 6 eggs
Seasonings of choice
Milk

2 to 3 corn tortillas, torn into
  bite-size pieces
Vegetable oil

Whisk the eggs and desired seasonings in a bowl until blended. Whisk in the
desired amount of milk. Fry the tortillas in a small amount of oil in a skillet; drain.
Return the tortillas to the skillet. Add the egg mixture and mix well. Cook until
the eggs are of the desired consistency, stirring frequently. Serve immediately.

Serves 3
Lynn Allen, Diamond Hill/Jarvis Branch

Cheese Grits

4 cups water
1 teaspoon salt
1 cup quick-cooking grits

8 ounces Velveeta cheese, melted
¼ cup (½ stick) margarine, melted
1 egg, lightly beaten

Bring the water and salt to a boil in a saucepan. Stir in the grits. Cook for 2 minutes. Add the cheese and margarine and mix well. Stir a small amount of the hot grits mixture into the egg. Stir the egg into the grits. Spoon the grits mixture into a greased baking dish. Bake at 350 degrees for 30 minutes or until light brown on top.

For a quick and easy way to melt the cheese and margarine, slice the margarine and place in the bottom of a microwave-safe dish. Cube the cheese and arrange on top of the butter. Microwave until melted. The butter will make the cheese slide out of the dish easier.

Serves 4
Cindy Olson, Southwest Regional Library

Naomi's Cheese Grits

A very special friend gave me this recipe over twenty years ago. I have tried other versions, however this is my family's favorite for brunch or dinner.

6 cups water
1½ cups grits
1 pound Velveeta cheese, cubed
¾ cup (1½ sticks) margarine,
    softened

2 teaspoons (or less) seasoned salt
6 to 10 drops of hot sauce
3 eggs, beaten

Bring the water to a boil in a saucepan. Stir in the grits. Boil for 5 minutes. Remove from heat. Stir in the cheese, margarine, salt and hot sauce. Stir a small amount of the hot mixture into the eggs. Stir the eggs into the grits mixture.

Spoon the grits mixture into a buttered 9×13-inch baking dish. Bake at 250 degrees for 1 hour.

Serves 6 to 8
Barbara M. Smith, Central Library (retired)

Granny Flournoy's Apple Roll

This recipe was published in a church cookbook in Lisbon, Arkansas. The proceeds from the sale of the cookbook financed the purchase of twelve stained glass windows. Give it a try!

PASTRY
2 refrigerated 9-inch pie pastries
2 cups applesauce
3/4 cup (1½ sticks) margarine
1 cup sugar
2 teaspoons cinnamon
Butter to taste
Sugar to taste

SAUCE
1 cup sugar
2½ tablespoons cornstarch
1/8 teaspoon salt
2 cups milk
3 tablespoons margarine
1 teaspoon vanilla extract

For the pastry, roll one of the pastries into a 12×12-inch square on a lightly floured surface. Spread 1 cup of the applesauce to within 1½ inches of the edges. Dot with half the margarine. Sprinkle with ½ cup of the sugar and 1 teaspoon of the cinnamon.

Starting on one side, fold the pastry to the center. Repeat the process on the opposite side. Tuck in the ends to form a rectangle. Arrange seam side down on a greased 9×13-inch baking sheet. Prick the top with a fork. Repeat the process with the remaining pastry, applesauce, margarine, sugar and cinnamon. Bake at 350 degrees for 45 minutes. Dot the rolls with butter and sprinkle with sugar to taste. Bake for 15 minutes longer.

For the sauce, combine the sugar, cornstarch and salt in a saucepan and mix well. Add the milk and margarine. Cook until the sauce begins to thicken, stirring frequently. Stir in the vanilla. Drizzle over the rolls.

Serves 8
Laura Cleveland, Watauga Public Library

Oatmeal Buttermilk Pancakes

2 cups buttermilk
1¼ cups old-fashioned oats
2 eggs, beaten, or ½ cup egg substitute
1 cup flour
3 tablespoons sugar
1 teaspoon baking soda
1 teaspoon salt
¼ cup vegetable oil

Combine the buttermilk and oats in a bowl and mix well. Stir in the eggs. Combine the flour, sugar, baking soda and salt in a bowl and mix well. Add to the oats mixture and mix well. Stir in the oil.

Pour ¼ cup of the batter at a time onto a hot lightly greased griddle. Reduce the heat to medium-low. Cook until bubbles appear around the edge; turn. Cook until light brown. Repeat the process with the remaining batter.

Serves 4 to 6
Linda Waggener, Floater

Chocolate Gravy

¾ cup sugar
1 tablespoon (rounded) baking cocoa
1 teaspoon flour
⅛ teaspoon salt
¼ cup evaporated milk
1 to 2 tablespoons butter
1 teaspoon vanilla extract

Combine the sugar, baking cocoa, flour and salt in a saucepan and mix well. Stir in the evaporated milk, butter and vanilla. Bring to a rolling boil over low heat, stirring constantly. Remove from heat. Serve over hot biscuits.

Serves 6 to 8
Wanda Cargill, Haltom City Public Library

DESSERTS, CANDY & COOKIES

des·sert (di·zûrt′) *n.*

A confection, such as soufflé,
served as the final course of a meal.

Shown above: Fort Worth Public Library on the corner of Throckmorton and 9th, across from City Hall, 1939-1978

Where to Find the Library

Central Library
500 W. 3rd Street
Est. 1901
Expansion 2000

2 Regional Libraries:

East Regional
6301 Bridge Street
Est. 1996

Southwest Regional
4001 Library Lane
Est. 1987

(continued on page 142)

A Bad Dream

I call this dessert a bad dream because I had a dream about a table covered with delicious foods. This dessert was on the table and caught my eye. It was beautiful, sparkling and shining. Just as I was about to put a bite of this dessert in my mouth, I awoke. So I decided to make the "bad dream" come true.

8 to 16 ounces cream cheese, softened
8 to 16 ounces whipped topping
2 to 3 cups sugar
1 teaspoon almond extract
1 (16-ounce) loaf pound cake
1 to 2 (16-ounce) cans sliced peaches
1 (16-ounce) package frozen sliced strawberries or
    blueberries, thawed
Whipped topping

Beat the desired amount of cream cheese, whipped topping and sugar in a mixing bowl at medium speed until smooth. Beat in the almond extract and set aside.

Cut the pound cake into 9 equal slices. Line the bottom of a clear glass dessert bowl with 3 of the cake slices. Layer evenly with ⅓ of the cream cheese mixture and half of the desired amount of undrained peaches. Top with half of the remaining cake slices. Layer with half of the remaining cream cheese mixture and half of the strawberries. Top with the remaining cream cheese mixture, remaining cake slices, remaining peaches and remaining strawberries. Spread with additional whipped topping. Chill, covered, until ready to serve.

Serves 8 to 10
Wynona F. Lee, Floater

Banana Split Cake

½ cup (1 stick) margarine, melted
2 cups graham cracker crumbs
1 cup (2 sticks) margarine, softened
2 eggs
1 (1-pound) package confectioners' sugar
6 bananas, thinly sliced

1 (8-ounce) can crushed pineapple, drained
12 ounces whipped topping
12 maraschino cherries, cut into halves
½ cup finely chopped pecans

Combine the melted margarine and graham cracker crumbs in a small bowl and mix well. Press the crumb mixture into a 9×13-inch dish. Combine the softened margarine, eggs and confectioners' sugar in a large mixing bowl. Beat at medium speed for exactly 10 minutes. Spread the creamed mixture in the prepared dish. Layer the bananas and pineapple over the prepared layer. Spread with the whipped topping. Top with the cherries and sprinkle with the pecans. Chill, covered, for 8 to 10 hours. Cut into squares.

Serves 15
Allison Long, Haltom City Public Library

Greater Than Sex Fruit Dessert

My mother and two of her sisters are diabetics. My cousin found this recipe to satisfy their sweet tooth. You do not have to be a diabetic to enjoy this dessert as my husband certainly did on one of our yearly journeys home. After he ate it, he questioned me as to why a dessert so good was called "grated insects!" Accents are funny sometimes.

1 angel food cake or sponge cake
2 small packages French vanilla sugar-free instant pudding mix
Sliced bananas

1 (8-ounce) can crushed pineapple, drained
Whipped cream or whipped topping
Chopped pecans to taste

Break the angel food cake into bite-size pieces. Prepare the pudding using package directions. Alternate layers of cake pieces, pudding, bananas and pineapple in a large square cake pan until all ingredients are used. Top with whipped cream and sprinkle with pecans. Use lesser amounts of whipped cream and pecans for diabetics. Chill, covered, for 8 to 10 hours or serve immediately. You may substitute strawberries for the pineapple in this recipe.

Serves 6 to 8
Lynn Allen, Diamond Hill/Jarvis Branch

Church Windows Dessert

You'll have many colored windows in each slice!

1 (3-ounce) package cherry gelatin
1 (3-ounce) package orange gelatin
1 (3-ounce) package lime gelatin
3 cups boiling water
1½ cups cold water
1 cup pineapple juice
¼ cup sugar
1 (3-ounce) package lemon gelatin
½ cup cold water
4 cups whipped topping
1½ tablespoons butter, melted
12 graham crackers, crushed

Dissolve the cherry gelatin, orange gelatin and lime gelatin each in separate square glass dishes in 1 cup of the boiling water, stirring constantly. Add ½ cup of the cold water to each of the three dishes and mix well. Chill, covered, until set.

Combine the pineapple juice and sugar in a small saucepan. Bring to a boil, stirring constantly. Remove from the heat and add the lemon gelatin, stirring until the gelatin dissolves. Stir in ½ cup cold water. Pour the mixture into a large bowl. Chill until mixture reaches the syrupy stage. Fold in the whipped topping. Cut the cherry, lime and orange gelatin into cubes. Fold the gelatin cubes into the lemon gelatin mixture.

Combine the butter and graham cracker crumbs in a small bowl and mix well. Press the mixture over the bottom and up the side of a greased 9-inch springform pan. Pour the gelatin mixture into the pan. Chill, covered, for 12 hours. Loosen the dessert from the side of the pan. Place on a serving plate and remove the side of the pan.

Serves 6 to 8
Eric Fry, Central Library

Gelatin
An odorless, tasteless and colorless thickening agent used for making molded desserts and salads. Before commercial gelatin was available, housewives boiled calves' feet or knuckles to make their own jelling agent.

Red Raspberry Russian Cream

My father got this recipe from the cafeteria where he worked as a security guard over thirty-five years ago. This creamy dessert was used at many special occasions and church potluck suppers. It was one of my dad's favorites.

2 cups heavy cream
2 cups sour cream
1³/₄ cups sugar
2 teaspoons vanilla extract

6¹/₄ teaspoons unflavored gelatin
³/₄ cup cold water
2 (10-ounce) packages frozen
    sweetened raspberries, thawed

Combine the heavy cream, sour cream, sugar and vanilla in a large bowl and stir (do not whip) until the sugar dissolves; set aside. Sprinkle the gelatin over the cold water in a small saucepan and let stand until the gelatin is softened. Heat over very low heat until the gelatin completely dissolves, stirring constantly. Add to the cream mixture and mix well. Pour into a 9×13-inch pan and chill until set. Cut into squares and serve topped with the raspberries.

Serves 10
Roberta Schenewerk, Central Library

Gena's Peachy Cheesecake

You may use any flavor of canned pie filling to top this cheesecake.

1¹/₃ cups graham cracker crumbs
¹/₂ teaspoon cinnamon
¹/₃ cup packed brown sugar
¹/₃ cup butter or margarine, melted
¹/₃ cup chopped pecans or almonds

32 ounces cream cheese, softened
1 cup sugar
1 teaspoon vanilla extract
4 small eggs, lightly beaten
1 (21-ounce) can peach pie filling

Combine the graham cracker crumbs, cinnamon, brown sugar, butter and pecans in a medium bowl and mix well. Press the mixture over the bottom and halfway up the side of a 10-inch springform pan. Bake at 325 degrees for 10 to 13 minutes or until golden brown. Remove to a wire rack to cool slightly.

    Combine the cream cheese, sugar, vanilla and eggs in a large mixing bowl and beat until smooth and creamy. Pour into the warm crust. Bake at 325 degrees for 1 hour or until the center is set. Cool in the pan on a wire rack. Chill for 4 hours to 10 hours. Loosen the cheesecake from the side of the pan. Place on a serving platter and remove the side of the pan. Top with the peach pie filling.

Serves 8
Gena Fisher, Central Library

The
Branches

Diamond Hill/
Jarvis Branch
1300 N.E. 35th Street
Est. 1989

East Berry Branch
4300 East Berry
Est. 1967

Meadowbrook Branch
5651 East
Lancaster Avenue
Est. 1964

Northside Branch
601 Park Street
Est. 1967

Ridglea Branch
3628 Bernie
Anderson Drive
Est. 1967

Riverside Branch
2913 Yucca Drive
Est. 1967

Seminary Branch
501 East Bolt Street
Est. 1967

Ella Mae
Shamblee Branch
959 East Rosedale St.
Est. 1982

Summerglen Branch
4205 Basswood Blvd.
Est. 2000

Wedgwood Branch
3816 Kimberly Lane
Est. 1962

(continued on
page 149)

Peppermint Mousse Cheesecake

This recipe won first place at the cheesecake cook-off. It is light and refreshing.

1 cup chocolate wafer crumbs
3 tablespoons margarine, melted
1 envelope unflavored gelatin
1/4 cup cold water
1/2 cup milk
1/4 cup crushed peppermint candies
16 ounces cream cheese, softened
1/2 cup sugar
8 ounces whipped topping
3 ounces milk chocolate, finely chopped

Combine the chocolate wafer crumbs and margarine in a small bowl and mix well. Press the crumb mixture over the bottom and halfway up the side of a 9-inch springform pan. Bake at 350 degrees for 10 minutes. Cool on a wire rack.

Stir the gelatin and water together in a small bowl and set aside. Heat the milk and crushed candies in a small saucepan over low heat until completely melted and smooth, stirring frequently. Add the gelatin mixture, stirring until the gelatin dissolves. Set the mixture aside to cool slightly.

Combine the cream cheese and sugar in a large mixing bowl and beat until smooth and creamy. Stir in the peppermint mixture. Chill for 30 minutes or until slightly thickened. Fold in the whipped topping and chocolate. Pour into the cooled crust. Chill until firm. Loosen the cheesecake from the side of the pan. Place the cheesecake on a serving platter and remove the side of the pan. Garnish with additional chocolate and crushed peppermint candies.

Serves 8
Roberta Schenewerk, Central Library

Mom's Upside-Down Apple Soufflé

My mother often made this dish Saturday mornings when I was growing up. As a child, I remember watching my mother standing over the kitchen sink slicing the peel off the apples in long continuous curls.

¼ cup (½ stick) margarine
¼ cup sugar
1 teaspoon cinnamon
5 medium apples, peeled, sliced
Juice of ½ lemon
¼ cup flour
¼ teaspoon baking powder
¼ teaspoon salt
¼ cup sugar
¼ cup milk
4 eggs yolks
4 egg whites, stiffly beaten

Melt the margarine in an 8- to 10-inch ovenproof skillet (not cast-iron) over low heat. Combine ¼ cup sugar and cinnamon in a small bowl and mix well. Sprinkle evenly over the margarine in the skillet and stir. Arrange the apple slices on top of the cinnamon mixture and drizzle with the lemon juice. Simmer over low heat for 10 minutes.

Sift the flour, baking powder and salt together. Combine ¼ cup sugar, milk and egg yolks in a large bowl and mix well. Add the sifted dry ingredients and mix well. Fold in the egg whites. Spoon the mixture over the apples in the skillet. Bake at 400 degrees for 30 minutes or until puffed and golden brown. Loosen and invert immediately onto a serving plate.

Serves 4
Melissa Speed, Central Library

Soufflé (soo·FLAY)
A light, airy mixture made with eggs that can be savory or sweet, hot or cold.

Apple Crunch

1 (21-ounce) can apple pie filling
½ cup raisins (optional)
1 (1-layer) package yellow or white
   cake mix

½ cup chopped pecans
½ cup (1 stick) margarine, melted

Layer the pie filling, raisins and cake mix evenly in a greased 8×8-inch baking dish. Sprinkle with the pecans. Drizzle with the margarine. Bake at 350 degrees for 45 minutes. Cool slightly before serving.

Serves 4
Lida Launius, Richland Hills Public Library

Cinnamon Nut Diamonds

A patron of Meadowbrook Library brought these to us every year during the Christmas season.

1 cup (2 sticks) butter, softened
1 cup packed brown sugar
1 teaspoon vanilla extract
1 egg yolk
½ teaspoon salt

1 teaspoon cinnamon
1 cup ground walnuts or pecans
1¾ to 2 cups flour
1 egg white, lightly beaten

Combine the butter, brown sugar, vanilla and egg yolk in a large mixing bowl and beat at medium speed until light and fluffy. Add the salt, cinnamon, half of the ground walnuts and enough of the flour to make of the desired consistency and mix well.

Spread the batter evenly in a greased 10×15-inch baking pan with sides. Brush with the egg white. Sprinkle with the remaining ground walnuts. Bake at 350 degrees for 25 to 30 minutes or at 275 degrees for 70 minutes or until golden brown. Cool and cut into 2-inch diamond shapes.

Serves 10
Frances Allen, Ella Mae Shamblee Branch

Peach Tortillas

You will have to try this. It is delicious served warm and very easy to prepare. You may substitute apples, pears, apricots or berries for the peaches in this recipe.

6 to 8 fresh peaches, peeled, sliced
Fruit-Fresh
10 large flour tortillas
1 cup (2 sticks) butter
2 cups sugar

1½ cups water
Sugar to taste
Cinnamon to taste
Nutmeg to taste

Sprinkle the peach slices with Fruit-Fresh. Divide the peach slices evenly among the flour tortillas. Roll to enclose the filling. Arrange the tortillas seam side down in a greased 9×13-inch baking pan.

Bring the butter, 2 cups sugar and water to a boil in a medium saucepan over medium heat, stirring constantly. Pour over the tortillas. Let stand for 45 minutes. Sprinkle evenly with sugar to taste, cinnamon and nutmeg. Bake at 350 degrees for 1 hour; do not overbake. Cool slightly on a wire rack. Serve warm.

Serves 10
Barbara M. Smith, Central Library (retired)

Homemade Ice Cream

To crank the ice cream machine, you will need children to start and strong adults to finish.

4 eggs
1 cup sugar
1 cup heavy cream
1 tablespoon vanilla extract

2 (14-ounce) cans sweetened
    condensed milk
Chopped fruit (optional)
6 cups (about) milk

Combine the eggs, sugar, heavy cream and vanilla in a large mixing bowl. Beat at medium speed until blended. Pour into an ice cream freezer container. Add the condensed milk and fruit and mix well. Add the milk to the fill line and stir until well mixed. Freeze using manufacturer's directions.

Makes 1 gallon
Karen Brown, Central Library

Texas Haystacks

1 pound almond bark, chopped
1 cup peanut butter Cap'n Crunch cereal
1 cup pretzel sticks
1 cup salted peanuts

Place the almond bark in a microwave-safe bowl. Microwave according to the package directions until the almond bark is melted and smooth, stirring occasionally. Stir in the cereal, pretzel sticks and peanuts. Drop by teaspoonfuls onto wax paper. Let stand until firm. Store in an airtight container.

Serves 4 to 6
Brenda Lanche, Riverside Branch

Potato Fudge

When I was nine years old, my mother found this recipe in the Fort Worth Star Telegram. *It was such an unusual idea so she thought she would try it. It tasted wonderful! What a delight to bring samples of this to school for Christmas parties and such. It also makes a great gift. Simply wrap in a decorated box or basket. This recipe is so simple, children can make it, with adult supervision of course.*

½ cup (1 stick) margarine
2 ounces unsweetened chocolate
¼ cup mashed cooked potatoes
1 (1-pound) package confectioners' sugar
Chopped pecans (optional)

Melt the margarine and chocolate in a small saucepan over low heat, stirring constantly. Add the potatoes and mix well. Pour the mixture into a medium mixing bowl. Add the confectioners' sugar gradually, mixing well after each addition.

Spread the potato mixture evenly in a greased 8×8-inch baking pan. Sprinkle with the pecans. Chill for 1 hour or longer. Cut into small squares to serve.

Serves 6 to 8
Allison Long, Haltom City Public Library

Buttermilk Pralines

2 cups sugar
1 teaspoon baking soda
1 cup buttermilk
2 teaspoons vanilla extract
2 cups pecan halves

Combine the sugar, baking soda and buttermilk in a medium saucepan and mix well. Cook over low heat until the sugar dissolves, stirring constantly. Cook over medium heat to 234 to 240 degrees on a candy thermometer, soft-ball stage, stirring constantly. Remove from heat and stir in the vanilla and pecans.

Beat vigorously until the mixture begins to thicken. Drop by teaspoonfuls onto waxed paper. Let stand until cool.

Makes 30 pralines
Betty Patterson, Richland Hills Public Library

Dr. Pepper Pralines

1 cup sugar
1 cup packed dark brown sugar
1 cup Dr. Pepper
4 large marshmallows
2 to 3 cups pecan halves or walnut halves

Combine the sugar, brown sugar and Dr. Pepper in a heavy saucepan and mix well. Cook over low heat until the sugars are completely dissolved, stirring constantly. Cook over high heat to 234 to 240 degrees on a candy thermometer, soft-ball stage, stirring occasionally. Remove from heat.

Stir in the marshmallows and pecans. Beat vigorously for 1 to 2 minutes or until thick and creamy. Drop by tablespoonfuls onto waxed paper. Let stand until cool.

Makes 30 to 40 pralines
Renée Cordray, Ridglea Branch

English Toffee

2 cups (4 sticks) butter
2 cups sugar
3 tablespoons water
1 cup slivered almonds
1 cup (6 ounces) semisweet chocolate chips
½ cup sliced almonds

Melt the butter in a medium saucepan over low heat. Add the sugar and water and mix well. Cook over low heat until the sugar dissolves, stirring constantly. Cook over medium heat to 250 degrees on a candy thermometer, firm-ball stage, stirring constantly. Remove from heat and stir in the slivered almonds.

Cook over medium heat to 300 degrees on a candy thermometer, hard-crack stage, stirring constantly. Spread in a greased 10×15-inch baking pan and sprinkle with the chocolate chips. Let stand until the chocolate begins to melt. Spread melted chips evenly over candy and sprinkle with the sliced almonds. Let stand until cool. Break into pieces.

Makes 2½ pounds
Cornelia Pim, Seminary South Branch

Brownies

1 cup (2 sticks) butter, softened
2 cups sugar
4 eggs
1⅓ cups flour
½ cup baking cocoa
1 cup chopped pecans or walnuts

Cream the butter and sugar in a large mixing bowl until light and fluffy. Add the eggs 1 at a time, mixing well after each addition. Sift the flour and baking cocoa together. Add to the creamed mixture and mix well. Stir in the pecans.

Pour the batter into a greased and floured 9×13-inch baking pan. Bake at 350 degrees for 30 minutes or until the brownies pull from the sides of the pan. Let stand until cool. Cut into squares.

Makes 2 dozen brownies
Lisa Harper Wood, Keller Public Library

Double-Fudge Brownies

The Double-Fudge Brownie mix recipe below will fill a 6-cup container and makes a great gift for a brownie lover. Instructions for preparing brownies using the dry mix should be attached to the gift.

DOUBLE-FUDGE BROWNIE MIX
2 cups sugar
1 cup baking cocoa (not Dutch process)
1 cup flour
1 cup chopped pecans
1 cup (6 ounces) chocolate chips

BROWNIES
1 cup (2 sticks) butter or margarine, softened
4 eggs

For the brownie mix, layer the ingredients in the order listed in an airtight container. Store in a cool dry place or freeze in a sealable plastic freezer bag. Makes 6 cups dry mix.

For the brownies, beat the butter in a large mixing bowl at medium speed until creamy. Add the eggs 1 at a time, beating well after each addition. Add 1 recipe Double-Fudge Brownie Mix and stir until well mixed.

Spread the chocolate mixture in a greased 9×13-inch baking pan. Bake at 325 degrees for 40 to 50 minutes or until brownies pull from the sides of the pan. Cool completely on a wire rack. Cut into squares.

Makes 2 dozen brownies
Karen Brown, Central Library

The Satellites and MetroPacs

Satellite Libraries located in public housing communities:

BOLD, Butler Outreach Library Butler Housing Community Est. 1997

COOL, Cavile Outreach Opportunity Library 5060 Avenue G. Est. 1994

MetroPac Libraries:

Haltom City Public Library 3201 Friendly Lane

Keller Public Library 640 Johnson Road

Richland Hills Public Library 6724 Rena Drive

Watauga Public Library 7109 Whitley Road

Blonde Brownies

2 cups flour
1 teaspoon baking powder
¼ teaspoon baking soda
1 teaspoon salt
⅔ cup butter or margarine

2 cups packed brown sugar
2 eggs, lightly beaten
2 teaspoons vanilla extract
1 cup (6 ounces) chocolate chips
⅓ cup chopped pecans or walnuts

Sift the flour, baking powder, baking soda and salt together. Melt the butter in a medium saucepan over low heat. Remove from heat. Add the brown sugar and mix well. Beat in the eggs and vanilla until smooth. Add the sifted dry ingredients gradually, mixing well after each addition.

Spread the batter in a greased 9×13-inch baking pan. Sprinkle evenly with the chocolate chips and pecans. Bake at 350 degrees for 30 minutes or until the brownies pull from the sides of the pan. Cool in the pan on a wire rack. Cut into bars.

Makes 2 dozen brownies
Karen Brown, Central Library

Can't Leave Alone Bars

1 (2-layer) package white cake mix
2 eggs, lightly beaten
⅓ cup vegetable oil
1 (14-ounce) can sweetened
　　condensed milk

1 cup (6 ounces) semisweet chocolate
　　chips
¼ cup (½ stick) butter or margarine,
　　sliced

Combine the cake mix, eggs and oil in a medium bowl and mix well. Pat ⅔ of the mixture into a greased 9×13-inch baking pan using floured hands. Set the remaining cake mixture aside.

Combine the condensed milk, chocolate chips and butter in a microwave-safe bowl. Microwave on High for 45 to 60 seconds or until chocolate chips and butter are melted. Remove from microwave and stir until smooth. Pour into the prepared baking pan. Drop the remaining cake mixture by teaspoonfuls evenly over the top. Bake at 350 degrees for 20 to 25 minutes or until light brown. Let stand until cool. Cut into bars.

Makes 3 dozen bars
Sylvia Autry, Wedgwood Branch

Chocolate Yummies

½ cup (1 stick) butter, melted
1½ cups graham cracker crumbs
1 (14-ounce) can sweetened
  condensed milk

½ cup (3 ounces) chocolate chips
½ cup shredded coconut
Chopped pecans (optional)

Layer the butter, graham cracker crumbs and condensed milk in a 9×13-inch baking pan. Sprinkle with the chocolate chips, coconut and pecans. Press the layers together lightly. Bake at 325 degrees for 25 to 30 minutes or until firm. Let stand until cool. Cut into squares.

Makes 2 dozen squares
Lida Launius, Richland Hills Public Library

Oatmeal Marble Squares

In high school, my twin sister, best friend and I (also known as the three musketeers) discovered this recipe and made it frequently for marching band and church parties. Twenty-five years later, this remains one of my favorite recipes because it is easy to make and is not overly sweet.

½ cup (1 stick) butter, softened
6 tablespoons sugar
½ teaspoon vanilla extract
¼ teaspoon (or more) water
1 egg, lightly beaten
¾ cup flour

½ teaspoon baking soda
½ teaspoon salt
1 cup rolled oats
½ cup chopped pecans
1 cup (6 ounces) chocolate chips

Cream the butter and sugar in a medium mixing bowl until light and fluffy. Add the vanilla, water and egg and mix until smooth. Sift the flour, baking soda and salt together. Add the sifted dry ingredients and the oats to the creamed mixture and mix well. Stir in the pecans.

Press the oats mixture into a greased 8×8-inch baking pan. Sprinkle with the chocolate chips. Bake at 350 degrees for 1 minute or until chocolate chips just begin to melt. Remove from the oven and swirl through the batter with a knife to marbleize. Bake for 12 to 14 minutes longer or until firm. Let stand until cool. Cut into squares.

Makes 2 dozen squares
Roberta Schenewerk, Central Library

Pecan Pie Bars

2 cups flour
1/2 cup sugar
1/8 teaspoon salt
1/4 cup (1/2 stick) butter, sliced
1 cup packed brown sugar
1 cup light corn syrup
1/2 cup (1 stick) butter
4 eggs, lightly beaten
2 1/2 cups finely chopped pecans
1 teaspoon vanilla extract

Combine the flour, sugar and salt in a large bowl. Cut in 1/4 cup butter until crumbly. Press the crumb mixture into a greased 9×13-inch baking pan. Bake at 350 degrees for 17 to 20 minutes or until light brown. Set aside to cool.

Bring the brown sugar, corn syrup and 1/2 cup butter to a boil in a medium saucepan over medium heat, stirring constantly. Remove from the heat and stir 1/4 of the hot mixture into the beaten eggs in a medium bowl. Add the egg mixture to the hot mixture and mix well. Stir in the pecans and vanilla. Pour evenly over the cooled crust. Bake at 350 degrees for 30 to 35 minutes or until set. Cool completely in the pan on a wire rack. Cut into bars.

Makes 16 large bars
Cornelia Pim, Seminary South Branch

Peanut Butter Bars

These taste like Reese's Peanut Butter Cups.

2 cups graham cracker crumbs
1 (1-pound) package confectioners' sugar
1 cup (2 sticks) margarine, softened
1½ cups creamy peanut butter
2 cups (12 ounces) chocolate chips, melted

Combine the graham cracker crumbs and confectioners' sugar in a large bowl and mix well. Combine the margarine and peanut butter in a medium mixing bowl and beat until smooth. Add to the confectioners' sugar mixture and mix well.

   Press the peanut butter mixture into a greased 9×13-inch dish. Pour the chocolate evenly over the top. Let stand until cool or chill before cutting into bars.

Makes 2 dozen bars
Frances Allen, Ella Mae Shamblee Branch

No-Bake Chocolate Cookies

¼ cup baking cocoa
2 cups sugar
½ cup (1 stick) butter, melted
½ cup milk
½ cup peanut butter
2 cups quick-cooking oats

Combine the baking cocoa, sugar, butter and milk in a large heavy saucepan and mix well. Bring to a rolling boil over high heat, stirring constantly. Remove from the heat and stir in the peanut butter and oats. Drop by tablespoonfuls onto waxed paper. Let stand until cool and firm.

Makes 2 to 3 dozen cookies
Linda Waggener, Floater

Fudge Peanut Oaties

2 cups sugar
3 tablespoons baking cocoa
1/2 cup (1 stick) margarine
1/2 cup milk
1/2 cup peanut butter
1 teaspoon vanilla extract
3 cups quick-cooking oats

Bring the sugar, baking cocoa, margarine and milk to a rolling boil in a large saucepan over medium-high heat, stirring constantly. Boil for 3 minutes, stirring constantly. Remove from heat and add the peanut butter and vanilla and mix well. Stir in the oats.

Drop by teaspoonfuls onto waxed paper. Let stand for 1 to 1 1/2 hours or until cool and set. Store in an airtight container.

Makes about 3 dozen cookies
Lida Launius, Richland Hills Public Library

Cookies While You Sleep

2 egg whites
1/8 teaspoon of salt
2/3 cup sugar
1 teaspoon vanilla extract
1/4 teaspoon almond extract
1 cup chopped pecans
1 cup (6 ounces) chocolate chips

Place the egg whites in a mixing bowl. Beat at high speed until soft peaks form. Add the salt. Add the sugar gradually, beating until stiff peaks form. Add the vanilla and almond extract and beat just until mixed. Fold in the pecans and chocolate chips.

Drop by teaspoonfuls onto a foil-lined cookie sheet. Place in a preheated 350-degree oven and turn off the oven. Let stand with the oven door closed for 8 to 10 hours or while you are sleeping; do not peek. Store in an airtight container.

Makes 2 dozen cookies
Frances Allen, Ella Mae Shamblee Branch

Chewy Gingersnaps

½ cup (1 stick) margarine, softened
⅔ cup sugar
½ cup molasses
1 egg, lightly beaten
2¾ cups flour
2 teaspoons baking soda
1 teaspoon ground ginger
½ teaspoon salt
½ teaspoon ground cloves
¾ teaspoon cinnamon
¼ cup finely chopped candied ginger
Sugar to taste

Cream the margarine and ⅔ cup sugar in a large mixing bowl until light and fluffy. Beat in the molasses and egg until well blended. Sift the flour, baking soda, ground ginger, salt, cloves and cinnamon together. Add the sifted dry ingredients to the creamed mixture gradually, mixing well after each addition. Fold in the candied ginger. Chill, covered, for 1 to 2 hours or until firm.

Shape the chilled dough by tablespoonfuls into balls. Dip half of each ball into sugar to taste and arrange sugar side up 3 inches apart on a greased cookie sheet. Bake at 350 degrees for 10 minutes. Cool on the cookie sheet for 2 minutes. Remove to a wire rack to cool completely.

Makes 4 dozen cookies
Roberta Schenewerk, Central Library

Ginger
The root of a tropical plant found predominately in Jamaica and means "horn root" in Sanskrit, referring to its gnarled bumpy appearance. Ground ginger is indispensable in gingerbread and spice cookies. Candied ginger has been cooked in sugar syrup and coated with coarse sugar.

Activities

The fifteen libraries in the Fort Worth Public Library System provide literacy-based programs for youths and adults. In addition to traditional preschool storytimes, the Library offers bilingual storytimes, homework tutoring, teen cafés, Cyber Senior training, and Adult Education classes. Local performers and nationally known authors and illustrators headline youth and adult programs. The branch and regional libraries can host small exhibits while the Central Library has a 7,000-square-foot gallery for art and music events.

(continued on page 158)

Israeli Honey Cookies

$1/2$ cup shortening
$1/2$ cup honey
1 egg
1 teaspoon vanilla extract
1 cup flour
1 teaspoon baking powder
$1/4$ teaspoon salt
$1/2$ cup rolled oats
1 cup chopped semisweet chocolate
$1/2$ cup chopped pecans or walnuts
$1/2$ cup golden raisins

Cream the shortening, honey, egg and vanilla in a large mixing bowl until light and fluffy. Sift the flour, baking powder and salt together. Add to the creamed mixture and mix well. Stir in the oats, chocolate, pecans and raisins.

Drop the dough by rounded teaspoonfuls 2 inches apart onto a greased cookie sheet. Bake at 375 degrees for 10 minutes. Cool on the cookie sheet for 2 minutes. Remove to a wire rack to cool completely.

Makes 2 dozen cookies
Sarah Harris, Riverside Branch

Mocha Truffle Cookies

These cookies have a soft, truffle-like center and a crispy outside.

¹/₂ cup (1 stick) margarine
¹/₂ cup (3 ounces) semisweet chocolate chips
1 tablespoon instant coffee granules
³/₄ cup sugar
³/₄ cup packed brown sugar
2 eggs, lightly beaten
2 teaspoons vanilla extract
2 cups flour
¹/₃ cup baking cocoa
¹/₂ teaspoon salt
1 teaspoon baking powder
1 cup (6 ounces) semisweet chocolate chips

Melt the margarine and ¹/₂ cup chocolate chips in a large heavy saucepan over low heat, stirring frequently. Stir in the coffee granules. Remove from heat. Let stand for 5 minutes. Add the sugar, brown sugar, eggs and vanilla and beat well. Sift the flour, baking cocoa, salt and baking powder together. Add the sifted dry ingredients to the chocolate mixture and blend well. Stir in 1 cup chocolate chips.

Drop the dough by tablespoonfuls 2 inches apart onto a greased cookie sheet. Bake at 350 degrees for 10 minutes. Cool on the cookie sheet for 1 minute. Remove to a wire rack to cool completely.

Makes 30 cookies
Roberta Schenewerk, Central Library

Mocha
Historically, a high-quality coffee grown in Arabia and shipped from Yemen's port of Mocha. Today, the term refers to food items with a coffee/chocolate flavor.

Molasses Crinkles

3/4 cup shortening, or 3/4 cup (1½ sticks) margarine, softened
1 cup packed brown sugar
1 egg, lightly beaten
¼ cup light molasses
2¼ cups flour
¼ teaspoon salt
2 teaspoons baking soda
1 teaspoon cinnamon
1 teaspoon ginger
½ teaspoon ground cloves
½ cup (or more) sugar

Cream the shortening and brown sugar in a mixing bowl until light and fluffy. Add the egg and molasses and beat well. Sift the flour, salt, baking soda, cinnamon, ginger and cloves together. Add the sifted dry ingredients to the creamed mixture and stir until smooth and well mixed. Chill, covered, for several hours.

Shape the dough into 1-inch balls. Roll in the sugar. Place 2 inches apart on an ungreased cookie sheet. Bake at 350 degrees for 12 to 15 minutes or until light brown. Cool on the cookie sheet for 1 minute. Remove to a wire rack to cool completely.

Makes about 3 dozen cookies
Sarah Harris, Riverside Branch

Pecan Cream Cheese Riches

I got this recipe from my sister over fifteen years ago. I like it because it is so versatile. It works with any flavor cake mix from white to spice to devil's food.

2/3 cup margarine, softened
8 ounces cream cheese, softened
2 egg yolks
2 teaspoons vanilla extract

1 (2-layer) package any flavor
  cake mix
2 cups chopped pecans
Confectioners' sugar

Cream the margarine and cream cheese in a large mixing bowl until light and fluffy. Add the egg yolks and vanilla and beat well. Stir in the cake mix and pecans. Chill, covered, for 1 hour.

Shape the dough into 1-inch balls. Place 2 inches apart on a greased cookie sheet. Bake at 350 degrees for 12 to 15 minutes or until light brown. Cool slightly and roll the warm cookies in confectioners' sugar.

Makes 4 dozen cookies
Roberta Schenewerk, Central Library

Scottish Shortcake Cookies

This recipe is over 100 years old and was passed down through our family by my husband's grandmother from Plean, Scotland. I make it every year the same way she made it.

8 ounces lard
1 (1-pound) package brown sugar

2 cups (4 sticks) butter, softened
12 cups flour

Combine the lard, brown sugar and butter in a very large mixing bowl and beat until smooth and creamy. Add the flour gradually, mixing well after each addition.

Roll small amounts of the dough 1/8 inch thick on a floured surface. Cut with a cookie cutter. Place 2 inches apart on a nonstick cookie sheet. Bake at 325 degrees for 25 minutes. Cool on a wire rack.

Makes 14 to 18 dozen cookies
Betty Patterson, Richland Hills Public Library

Snowflakes

1 cup shortening
3 ounces cream cheese, softened
1 cup sugar
1 egg yolk
1 teaspoon vanilla extract
1 teaspoon finely grated orange zest
2½ cups flour
½ teaspoon salt
¼ teaspoon cinnamon
Colored sugar
Cinnamon and sugar
Chopped almonds

Cream the shortening and cream cheese in a mixing bowl until light and fluffy. Add the sugar gradually, mixing well after each addition. Add the egg yolk, vanilla and orange zest and beat well. Sift the flour, salt and cinnamon together. Add the sifted dry ingredients to the creamed mixture and mix well.

Place the dough in a cookie press fitted with the desired tip. Press onto an ungreased cookie sheet. Decorate as desired with colored sugar, cinnamon and sugar and/or chopped almonds. Bake at 350 degrees for 12 to 15 minutes or until light brown. Remove immediately to a wire rack to cool.

Makes 3 to 4 dozen cookies
Sarah Harris, Riverside Branch

CAKES & PIES

pie (pi) *n.*

A baked food having a sweet or savory filling
prepared in a pasty-lined dish.

Shown above: Carnegie Public Library, Interior, 1901-1938

Carrot Cake

CAKE
2¼ cups flour
1½ cups sugar
2 tablespoons baking soda
1½ teaspoons cinnamon
½ teaspoon nutmeg
½ teaspoon salt
3 eggs, lightly beaten
1 cup vegetable oil
½ cup milk
2 cups shredded carrots
1½ cups flaked coconut
¼ cup chopped walnuts
½ cup raisins

CREAM CHEESE FROSTING
8 ounces cream cheese, softened
2 tablespoons butter, softened
2 tablespoons milk
½ teaspoon vanilla extract
⅛ teaspoon salt
2 to 2¼ cups confectioners' sugar

For the cake, combine the flour, sugar, baking soda, cinnamon, nutmeg and salt in a large mixing bowl and mix well. Whisk the eggs, oil and milk in a medium bowl until smooth. Add the egg mixture to the dry ingredients and beat at low speed until smooth. Stir in the carrots, coconut, walnuts and raisins. Pour the batter into a greased and floured 9×13-inch cake pan. Bake at 325 degrees for 55 to 60 minutes or until the cake tests done. Cool in the pan on a wire rack.

For the frosting, combine the cream cheese, butter, milk, vanilla and salt in a mixing bowl and beat until smooth and creamy. Add enough confectioners' sugar to make of spreading consistency. Spread over the top of the cake.

Serves 15
Brenda McCrary, Richland Hills Public Library

Pineapple Carrot Cake

CAKE
2 cups flour
2 cups sugar
2 teaspoons baking soda
2 teaspoons cinnamon
1 teaspoon salt
4 eggs, lightly beaten
1½ cups vegetable oil
2 (6-ounce) jars strained baby food carrots
1 (8-ounce) can crushed pineapple, drained
½ cup chopped pecans

CREAM CHEESE FROSTING
8 ounces cream cheese, softened
½ cup (1 stick) margarine, softened
1 teaspoon vanilla extract
3¾ cups (about) confectioners' sugar

For the cake, combine the flour, sugar, baking soda, cinnamon and salt in a large mixing bowl and mix well. Add the eggs, oil and carrots and beat at low speed until well mixed. Stir in the pineapple and pecans. Pour into 2 greased and floured 9-inch cake pans. Bake at 350 degrees for 35 to 40 minutes or until a wooden pick inserted in the center comes out clean. Cool in the pans for 10 minutes. Remove to a wire rack to cool completely.

For the frosting, beat the cream cheese and margarine in a medium bowl until smooth. Add the vanilla and mix well. Add enough confectioners' sugar to make of spreading consistency. Spread the frosting between the layers and over the top and side of the cake.

Serves 12
Sylvia Autrey, Wedgwood Branch

Darn Good Chocolate Cake

1 (2-layer) package devil's food
   cake mix
1 (4-ounce) package chocolate instant
   pudding mix
4 eggs, lightly beaten

1 cup sour cream
1/2 cup warm water
1/2 cup vegetable oil
1 1/2 cups (9 ounces) semisweet
   chocolate chips

Combine the cake mix, pudding mix, eggs, sour cream, water and oil in a large mixing bowl and beat at low speed for 1 minute, scraping the side of the bowl occasionally. Beat at medium speed for 2 to 3 minutes longer or until smooth and thoroughly mixed, scraping the side again if necessary. Fold in the chocolate chips.

   Pour the batter evenly into a greased and floured 12-cup bundt pan. Bake at 350 degrees for 45 to 50 minutes or until the cake springs back when lightly pressed with a finger and just starts to pull away from the side of the pan. Cool in the pan for 20 minutes. Invert onto a wire rack to cool completely. Frost as desired.

Serves 16
Renée Cordray, Ridglea Branch

Hershey Bar Cake

1 cup (2 sticks) butter or margarine,
   softened
2 cups sugar
5 eggs
3 (1 1/2-ounce) milk chocolate Hershey
   bars, melted

2 tablespoons baking cocoa
3 cups sifted flour
1 tablespoon baking powder
1 1/4 cups milk
1 teaspoon vanilla extract

Cream the butter and sugar in a large mixing bowl until light and fluffy. Add the eggs 1 at a time, mixing well after each addition. Add the melted candy bars and baking cocoa and beat well. Sift the flour and baking powder together. Add the dry ingredients and milk alternately to the creamed mixture, mixing well after each addition and beginning and ending with the dry ingredients. Stir in the vanilla.

   Pour the batter into 2 greased and floured 9-inch round cake pans. Bake at 350 degrees for 25 minutes or until a wooden pick inserted in the centers comes out clean. Cool in the pans for 10 minutes. Remove to a wire rack to cool completely. Frost as desired.

Serves 12
Pearlie Miller, East Berry Branch

Quick Cinnamon Nut Cake

This is a moist cake that can be topped with a dollop of whipped cream.

1 (2-layer) package yellow cake mix
3 eggs
1⅓ cups water
¼ cup vegetable oil
1¼ cups finely chopped pecans
7½ teaspoons sugar
4½ teaspoons cinnamon

Combine the cake mix, eggs, water and oil in a large mixing bowl and beat at medium speed for 2 minutes or until well blended. Combine the pecans, sugar and cinnamon in a small bowl and mix well. Sprinkle ⅓ of the pecan mixture evenly over the bottom of a greased 10-inch fluted tube pan. Layer with half the cake batter and half of the remaining pecan mixture. Repeat the layers with the remaining cake batter and the remaining pecan mixture.

Bake at 350 degrees for 35 to 40 minutes or until a wooden pick inserted near the center comes out clean. Cool in the pan for 10 minutes. Invert onto a wire rack to cool completely. Place cooled cake on a serving plate and top with whipped cream as above or frost as desired.

Serves 16
Sylvia Autrey, Wedgwood Branch

Cinnamon
A spice once used in love potions is made from the inner bark of a tropical evergreen tree. It is most commonly sold as cinnamon sticks, or ground into powder.

Coca-Cola Cake

CAKE
1½ cups sugar
1 cup vegetable oil
2 eggs, lightly beaten
2 ounces unsweetened chocolate, melted
1¾ cups flour
1 teaspoon baking soda
¾ cup Coca Cola

MINUTE-FUDGE ICING
1 cup sugar
⅓ cup evaporated milk
¼ cup (½ stick) margarine
1 ounce unsweetened chocolate
1 teaspoon vanilla extract

For the cake, combine the sugar and oil in a medium mixing bowl and mix well. Add the eggs and melted chocolate and beat well. Sift the flour and baking soda together. Add to the chocolate mixture and stir just until moistened. Add the cola and mix well. Pour into a greased 9×13-inch cake pan. Bake at 350 degrees for 30 to 35 minutes or until the cake tests done. Cool in the pan on a wire rack.

For the icing, bring the sugar, evaporated milk, margarine and chocolate to a boil in a small saucepan over medium heat, stirring constantly. Boil for 1 minute, stirring constantly. Remove from the heat and beat until lukewarm. Add the vanilla and beat for 1 minute or until smooth. Spread over the top of the cake.

Serves 15
Karen Brown, Central Library

Mildred's Coconut Cake

This was my father's favorite cake. It still makes me a smile to remember how his face would light up whenever he had one of these cakes. This cake was first given to him by a dear family friend, Mildred, for his birthday. He asked her to bake others for him over a period of time. One day Mildred shared the recipe with my mother, and now I share it with you. But the one thing you must not leave out when you make it is the spoonful of love that makes it irresistible and beautiful.

12 ounces whipped topping
2 cups sour cream
1 (14-ounce) package flaked coconut
1½ cups sugar
1 (2-layer) package butter-recipe cake mix

Combine the whipped topping, sour cream, coconut and sugar in a large mixing bowl and mix well. Chill, covered, for 8 to 10 hours. Prepare and bake the cake mix using package directions for a 2-layer 9-inch cake. Cool in the pans for 10 minutes. Remove to a wire rack to cool completely.

Slice each layer horizontally into halves. Spread the frosting between layers and over the top and side of the cake. Store, covered, in the refrigerator until serving time.

Serves 12
Brenda Lanche, Riverside Branch

Librarians Who Made a Difference

These Librarians made a commitment to make a difference in their community. The American Library Association and/or Texas Library Association have recognized most of these people. The American Library Association is "the voice of America's Libraries and provides leadership for the development, promotion, and improvement of library and information services and the profession of librarianship in order to enhance learning and ensure access to information for all." The Texas Library Association was established in 1902 to promote and improve library services in Texas.

(continued on page 169)

Cranberry Sauce Cake

3 cups flour
1½ cups sugar
1 cup mayonnaise
1 (16-ounce) can whole cranberry sauce
⅓ cup orange juice
1 tablespoon grated orange zest
1 teaspoon baking soda
1 teaspoon salt
1 teaspoon orange extract
1 cup chopped pecans
1 cup dried cranberries
1 cup confectioners' sugar
1½ tablespoons (or more) orange juice

Line the bottom of a greased 10-inch tube pan with greased waxed paper. Combine the flour, sugar, mayonnaise, cranberry sauce, ⅓ cup orange juice, orange zest, baking soda, salt and orange extract in a large bowl and mix well. Fold in the pecans and cranberries.

Pour the batter into the prepared pan. Bake at 350 degrees for 60 to 70 minutes or until the cake tests done. Cool in the pan for 10 minutes. Invert onto a serving plate and remove the waxed paper.

Combine the confectioners' sugar and 1½ tablespoons orange juice in a small bowl and mix until of a glaze consistency, adding additional orange juice if needed. Drizzle over the warm cake.

Serves 16
Roberta Schenewerk, Central Library

Cranberry
Grown in huge, sandy bogs on low, trailing vines in the northern climates of North America. They are sometimes called "bounceberries" because they bounce when ripe.

Cream Cheese Cake

1 cup (2 sticks) margarine, softened
½ cup (1 stick) butter, softened
8 ounces cream cheese, softened
3 cups sugar
6 eggs
3 cups sifted cake flour
2 teaspoons vanilla extract

Combine the margarine, butter and cream cheese in a large mixing bowl and beat at medium speed until smooth and creamy, scraping the bowl occasionally. Add the sugar gradually, beating at low speed. Beat for 5 minutes or until light and fluffy. Add the eggs 1 at a time, beating well after each addition. Add the flour and mix well. Stir in the vanilla.

Pour the batter into a greased 10-inch tube pan. Bake at 325 degrees for 1½ hours or until the cake tests done. Cool in the pan for 10 minutes. Invert onto a serving plate and cool completely. Frost as desired. Do not substitute margarine for the ½ cup butter in this recipe.

Serves 16
Pearlie Miller, East Berry Branch

Librarians, continued

Linda Allmand, Seventh Director, Fort Worth Public Library

Bob Bullock, former Lieutenant Governor of Texas

Laura Bush, First Lady of the United States of America, Texas Librarian, established the Texas Book Festival

Elizabeth Crabb, Coordinator, Northeast Texas Library System

Henry Cuellar, Texas State Representative

(continued on page 173)

Golden Fruit Cake

2 (6-ounce) packages dried apricots, chopped
1 cup chopped candied orange peel
1 (15-ounce) package golden raisins
1 cup coarsely chopped walnuts
½ cup brandy
2 cups (4 sticks) butter, softened
3 cups sugar
9 egg yolks, lightly beaten
5 cups flour
1 teaspoon salt
1 cup milk
2 teaspoons vanilla extract
9 egg whites
1 teaspoon cream of tartar

Line the bottoms of 3 greased 4×8-inch loaf pans with waxed paper. Combine the apricots, orange peel, raisins, walnuts and brandy in a large bowl and set aside for several hours.

Cream the butter and sugar in a large mixing bowl until light and fluffy. Beat in the egg yolks gradually. Sift the flour and salt together. Add the sifted dry ingredients to the creamed mixture alternately with the milk and vanilla, blending well after each addition. Beat the egg whites and cream of tartar in a medium bowl at high speed until stiff but not dry peaks form. Add the fruit mixture to the batter and mix well. Fold in the stiffly beaten egg whites.

Divide the batter evenly among the prepared pans. Place a pan of water on the bottom oven rack. Place the loaf pans on the middle oven rack. Bake at 275 degrees for 2 to 2½ hours or until the loaves test done. Cool in the pans on a wire rack. Remove loaves from pans, wrap in plastic wrap and place in sealable plastic bags. Store in a cool place or in the refrigerator for easy slicing.

Makes 3 loaves
Linda Waggener, Floater

Cream of tartar
A fine white powder made from a crystalline acid deposited on the inside of wine barrels. It can be added to candy and frosting mixtures for a creamier consistency and to egg whites before beating to improve stability.

Meyer Crumb Cake

2 cups packed brown sugar
2 cups flour
½ cup (1 stick) butter or margarine
1 cup buttermilk

1 teaspoon baking soda
1 egg
1 teaspoon vanilla extract

Combine the brown sugar and flour in a large bowl and mix well. Cut in the butter until crumbly. Reserve 1 cup of the crumb mixture. Add the buttermilk, baking soda, egg and vanilla to the remaining crumb mixture and mix well.

Pour the batter into a 9×13-inch cake pan and sprinkle evenly with the reserved crumb mixture. Bake at 350 degrees for 30 minutes. Let stand until cool. Cut into squares.

Serves 15
Betty Howe, Keller Public Library

Piña Colada Cake

1 (2-layer) package yellow cake mix
1 (4-ounce) package vanilla instant
  pudding mix
3 eggs, lightly beaten
¼ cup vegetable oil
1 cup water
1 (15-ounce) can cream of coconut

1 (14-ounce) can sweetened
  condensed milk
1 (20-ounce) can crushed pineapple,
  drained
8 ounces whipped topping
Flaked coconut to taste

Combine the cake mix and pudding mix in a large bowl and mix well. Add the eggs, oil and water and mix well. Bake using the package directions for a 9×13-inch cake pan. Cool in the pan on a wire rack for 10 minutes.

Combine the cream of coconut, condensed milk and crushed pineapple in a medium bowl and mix well. Pierce the surface of the warm cake evenly with a fork. Spread with the cream of coconut mixture. Chill, covered, for 2 to 3 hours.

Spread the chilled cake evenly with the whipped topping and sprinkle with flaked coconut. Cut into squares to serve. Store in the refrigerator.

Serves 15
Hilda Olson, Central Library

Pineapple Cream Cake

1 (2-layer) package yellow cake mix
1 (20-ounce) can crushed pineapple
Whipped topping

Prepare and bake the cake mix using the package directions for a 9×13-inch cake pan. Cool in the pan on a wire rack. Pierce the surface of the cake at 1-inch intervals with a fork. Spread the undrained crushed pineapple over the cake. Top with whipped topping. Chill, covered, for 24 hours. Cut into squares and serve. Store in the refrigerator.

Serves 15
Frances Allen, Ella Mae Shamblee Branch

Pound Cakes

2 cups (4 sticks) butter, softened
2 cups sugar
9 eggs
4 cups flour
1/2 teaspoon cream of tartar
1/2 teaspoon salt
2 tablespoons brandy

Cream the butter and sugar in a large mixing bowl until light and fluffy. Add the eggs 1 at a time, beating well after each addition. Sift the flour, cream of tartar and salt together. Add to the creamed mixture and mix well. Stir in the brandy.

Pour the batter into 2 greased 5×9-inch loaf pans. Bake at 325 degrees for 70 minutes or until a wooden pick inserted in the center comes out clean. Cool in the pans for 10 minutes. Remove to a wire rack to cool completely.

Makes 2 loaves
Pearlie Miller, East Berry Branch

Geranium Pound Cake

The name of this cake is derived from the rose geranium leaves (pelargonium graveolens) that may be used to line the pan before filling with the batter. The addition of geranium adds a strong "rose geranium" flavor to the finished cake.

1 cup (2 sticks) butter or margarine, softened
2 cups sugar
3 eggs
3 cups flour
2 teaspoons baking powder
1 cup milk
1 teaspoon vanilla extract
Rose geranium leaves (optional)
Confectioners' sugar (optional)

Cream the butter and sugar in a large bowl until light and fluffy. Add the eggs 1 at a time, mixing well after each addition. Sift the flour and baking powder together. Add to the creamed mixture alternately with the milk, mixing well after each addition and beginning and ending with the flour mixture. Stir in the vanilla.

Line the bottom of a greased 10-inch tube pan with geranium leaves. Pour the batter into the prepared pan. Bake at 350 degrees for 1 hour or until the cake tests done. Cool in the pan for 15 minutes. Invert onto a serving plate and sprinkle with confectioners' sugar.

Serves 16
Pearlie Miller, East Berry Branch

*(continued on
page 175)*

Lemonade Pound Cake

As this is a very rich and tart cake, serve it in small slices. Its texture has been compared to that of cheesecake.

1 (2-layer) package white cake mix
3 eggs
1 cup sour cream
3 ounces cream cheese, softened
1 (12-ounce) can frozen lemonade concentrate, thawed
2¼ cups (about) confectioners' sugar

Combine the cake mix, eggs, sour cream, cream cheese and half of the lemonade concentrate in a large mixing bowl and mix at low speed until moistened. Beat at high speed for 4 minutes.

Pour the batter into a greased and floured 10-inch tube pan. Bake at 350 degrees for 55 minutes or until the cake tests done. Cool in the pan for 10 minutes. Invert onto a serving plate and cool completely.

Mix the remaining lemonade concentrate with enough of the confectioners' sugar in a bowl to make of a glaze consistency. Drizzle the glaze evenly over the cooled cake. Slice to serve.

Serves 16
Roberta Schenewerk, Central Library

Pecan-Topped Chocolate Pound Cake

1 cup (2 sticks) butter or margarine, softened
½ cup shortening
2½ cups sugar
5 eggs
3 cups flour
½ cup baking cocoa
1 cup milk
1 cup chopped pecans

Cream the butter and shortening in a large mixing bowl until light. Add the sugar gradually, mixing until incorporated. Add the eggs 1 at a time, mixing well after each addition. Sift the flour and baking cocoa together. Add to the creamed mixture alternately with the milk, mixing well after each addition and beginning and ending with the flour mixture.

Pour the batter into a greased 10-inch tube pan and sprinkle evenly with the pecans. Bake at 325 degrees for 1¼ hours or until the cake tests done. Cool in the pan for 15 minutes. Invert onto a serving plate and cool completely.

Serves 16
Pearlie Miller, East Berry Branch

Gypsy Round Layer Cake

3/4 cup (1½ sticks) margarine, softened
1½ cups sugar
3 eggs
1¾ cups all-purpose flour, or 2 cups cake flour
1 teaspoon baking powder
½ teaspoon baking soda
½ teaspoon salt
2 tablespoons baking cocoa
1 teaspoon cinnamon
3/4 teaspoon nutmeg
3/4 cup buttermilk
1 teaspoon vanilla extract
1 teaspoon lemon extract
½ cup chopped pecans (optional)
1 recipe mocha icing

Cream the margarine and sugar in a large mixing bowl until light and fluffy. Add the eggs 1 at a time, mixing well after each addition. Sift the flour, baking powder, baking soda, salt, baking cocoa, cinnamon and nutmeg together. Add to the creamed mixture alternately with the buttermilk, vanilla and lemon extract, mixing well after each addition. Stir in the pecans.

Pour the batter into 2 greased and floured 9-inch cake pans. Bake at 350 degrees for 20 to 25 minutes or until the layers test done. Cool in the pans for 10 minutes. Remove to a wire rack to cool completely. Frost with your favorite mocha icing.

Serves 12
Sarah Harris, Riverside Branch

Red Devil's Food Cake

2¼ cups plus 2 tablespoons flour
1½ cups sugar
2 teaspoons baking soda
1 teaspoon salt
½ cup baking cocoa
¾ cup shortening
1½ cups milk
1½ teaspoons vanilla extract
3 eggs
1 recipe fluffy white icing

Sift the flour, sugar, baking soda, salt and baking cocoa into a mixing bowl and mix well. Add the shortening, milk and vanilla and beat at medium speed for 2 minutes or until smooth. Add the eggs and beat for 2 minutes longer or until smooth.

Pour the batter into 2 greased and floured 8-inch cake pans. Bake at 350 degrees for 30 to 35 minutes or until the layers test done. Cool in the pans for 10 minutes. Remove the layers to a wire rack to cool completely. Frost with your favorite fluffy white icing.

Serves 12
Becky Deaton, Haltom City Public Library

Sheath Cake

CAKE
2 cups flour
2 cups sugar
1 teaspoon baking soda
½ cup buttermilk
1 cup (2 sticks) margarine
6 tablespoons baking cocoa
1 cup water
2 eggs, lightly beaten
1 teaspoon cinnamon
1 teaspoon vanilla extract

CHOCOLATE PECAN FROSTING
½ cup (1 stick) margarine
¼ cup baking cocoa
6 tablespoons milk
1 (1-pound) package confectioners' sugar
1 teaspoon vanilla extract
1 cup chopped pecans

For the cake, combine the flour and sugar in a large mixing bowl and mix well. Dissolve the baking soda in the buttermilk in a small bowl and set aside. Melt the margarine in a small saucepan over medium heat. Stir in the baking cocoa and water. Bring to a boil, stirring constantly. Add the chocolate mixture to the flour mixture and mix well. Add the eggs, buttermilk mixture, cinnamon and vanilla and beat until smooth. Pour the batter into a 9×13-inch cake pan. Bake at 400 degrees for 25 minutes or until the cake tests done.

For the frosting, melt the margarine in a small saucepan over medium heat. Add the baking cocoa and bring the mixture to a boil, stirring constantly. Remove from heat. Stir in the milk, confectioners' sugar and vanilla. Add the pecans and mix well. Pour over the cake immediately upon removal from the oven. Let stand until cool. Cut into squares.

Serves 15
Lida Launius, Richland Hills Public Library

Sweet Potato Cake

CAKE
4 egg whites
2 cups sugar
1½ cups vegetable oil
4 egg yolks, lightly beaten
¼ cup hot water
1 teaspoon vanilla extract
2½ cups flour
1 tablespoon baking powder
¼ teaspoon salt
1 teaspoon cinnamon
1½ cups grated sweet potatoes
1 cup chopped pecans

COCONUT VANILLA ICING
1 (12-ounce) can evaporated milk
½ cup (1 stick) butter
3 egg yolks, lightly beaten
1½ cups sugar
1 teaspoon vanilla extract
1 cup shredded coconut

For the cake, beat the egg whites in a small bowl until stiff but not dry peaks form. Combine the sugar and oil in a large mixing bowl and mix well. Beat in the egg yolks. Blend in the water and vanilla until smooth. Sift the flour, baking powder, salt and cinnamon together. Add to the creamed mixture and mix well. Stir in the sweet potatoes and pecans. Fold in the stiffly beaten egg whites. Pour the batter into a greased and floured 9×13-inch cake pan. Bake at 325 degrees for 20 to 30 minutes or until the cake tests done. Cool in the pan on a wire rack.

For the icing, combine the evaporated milk, butter, egg yolks, sugar and vanilla in a medium saucepan and mix well. Cook over low heat for 12 minutes or until thickened, stirring constantly. Remove from the heat and stir in the coconut. Spread over the top of the cooled cake.

Serves 15
Marion Edwards, Riverside Branch

Seven-Up Cake

1 cup (2 sticks) butter or margarine, softened
3 cups sugar
5 eggs
3 cups flour
1 teaspoon vanilla extract
3/4 cup Seven-Up
1 cup confectioners' sugar
3 tablespoons vanilla extract

Cream the butter and sugar in a large mixing bowl until light and fluffy. Add the eggs 1 at a time, mixing well after each addition. Add the flour and 1 teaspoon vanilla and mix well. Fold in the soda.

Pour the batter into a greased 12-cup bundt pan. Bake at 325 degrees for 1 1/4 hours or until the cake tests done. Cool in the pan for 10 minutes. Invert onto a serving plate. Blend the confectioners' sugar and 3 tablespoons vanilla in a small bowl until smooth and of pouring consistency. Drizzle over the warm cake.

Serves 16
Karen Brown, Central Library

Brown Sugar Frosting

1/4 cup (1/2 stick) butter or margarine
1 1/2 cups sifted confectioners' sugar
1/2 cup packed brown sugar
2 tablespoons milk
1/2 teaspoon vanilla extract

Combine the butter, confectioners' sugar, brown sugar and milk in a medium saucepan and mix well. Cook over low heat until the butter melts and the confectioners' sugar and brown sugar dissolve, stirring constantly. Remove from heat. Add the vanilla, beating until smooth and of the desired spreading consistency.

Makes 1 1/2 cups
Pearlie Miller, East Berry Branch

Fluffy White Frosting

1 cup sugar
½ cup light corn syrup
¼ cup water

2 egg whites, at room temperature
1 teaspoon vanilla extract

Combine the sugar, corn syrup and water in a heavy saucepan and mix well. Cook over medium heat to 234 to 240 degrees on a candy thermometer, soft-ball stage, stirring constantly. Beat the egg whites at low speed in a mixing bowl until foamy. Pour the hot syrup mixture into the egg whites in a slow steady stream, beating constantly at medium speed. Beat at high speed until stiff peaks form and the frosting reaches the desired spreading consistency. Add the vanilla and beat until well blended. Spread immediately on any cooled cake.

Makes enough for one 2-layer cake
Pearlie Miller, East Berry Branch

Coconut Raisin Pecan Frosting

½ cup (1 stick) butter or margarine,
  softened
8 ounces cream cheese, softened
1 (1-pound) package confectioners'
  sugar, sifted

½ cup raisins, chopped
½ cup flaked coconut
½ cup chopped pecans
1 teaspoon vanilla extract

Beat the butter and cream cheese in a large mixing bowl until light and fluffy. Add the confectioners' sugar gradually, beating well after each addition. Stir in the raisins, coconut, pecans and vanilla and mix until of the desired spreading consistency. Use to frost a 9×13-inch cake or a 9-inch layer cake.

Makes about 3 cups
Pearlie Miller, East Berry Branch

Cherry Cream Cheese Pie

8 ounces cream cheese, softened
1 (14-ounce) can sweetened condensed milk
1/3 cup fresh lemon juice
1 tablespoon vanilla extract
1 (9-inch) graham cracker pie shell
1 (21-ounce) can cherry pie filling

Beat the cream cheese in a medium mixing bowl until smooth and creamy. Add the condensed milk, lemon juice and vanilla and blend well. Pour into the pie shell. Chill, covered, for 8 to 10 hours. Spread evenly with the cherry pie filling.

Serves 6 to 8
Lisa Harper Wood, Keller Public Library

Key Lime Pie

1 (14-ounce) can sweetened condensed milk
1/2 cup fresh Key lime juice
8 ounces whipped topping
1 (9-inch) graham cracker pie shell

Combine the condensed milk, lime juice and whipped topping in a medium bowl and blend until smooth and creamy. Pour into the pie shell. Chill, covered, for 8 to 10 hours.

Serves 6
Lida Launius, Richland Hills Public Library

Key lime
Grown only in Florida, the Key lime is smaller and rounder than the more widely available Persian lime. Its most popular use is in the famous Key lime pie.

Classic Walnut Pie

1 cup sugar
2 tablespoons flour
3 eggs, lightly beaten
1 cup light or dark corn syrup
2 tablespoons butter, melted
1 teaspoon vanilla extract
1 unbaked (9-inch) pie shell
1½ cups coarsely chopped walnuts

Combine the sugar and flour in a bowl and mix well. Add the eggs, corn syrup, butter and vanilla and mix well. Pour into the pie shell and sprinkle evenly with the walnuts.

Bake the pie on the oven rack in the lower third of the oven at 400 degrees for 15 minutes. Reduce the oven temperature to 350 degrees. Bake for 35 to 45 minutes longer or until firm. Remove to a wire rack to cool completely.

Serves 8
Karen Brown, Central Library

Joe's Yogurt Pie

8 ounces low-fat fruit-flavored yogurt
8 ounces whipped topping
1 (9-inch) graham cracker pie shell

Combine the yogurt and whipped topping in a medium bowl and fold together gently. Pour into the pie shell, spreading evenly. Chill, covered, for 1 hour or longer.

Serves 6
Mary Ann Prince, Central Library

Basic Pastry

1 cup all-purpose flour
1/2 teaspoon salt
1/2 cup plus 1 tablespoon chilled shortening
1 to 2 tablespoons ice water

Combine the flour and salt in a bowl. Cut in the shortening until the mixture is crumbly. Add the ice water 1 tablespoon at a time, mixing with a fork until the mixture forms a ball. Chill, wrapped in plastic wrap, for 30 minutes or longer.

Flatten dough into a disk on a lightly floured pastry cloth. Roll the dough from the center outward in all directions, using a lightly floured cloth-covered rolling pin. Lift the rolling pin as you near the edge on each stroke to achieve an even thickness. Roll to a 1/8- to 1/4-inch thickness, 1 1/2 inches larger in diameter than the pie plate. Fit the rolled dough into the pie plate, flute the edges and fill as desired. Bake as pie recipe indicates.

Makes 1 (9-inch) pie shell
Pearlie Miller, East Berry Branch

Easy Piecrust

1 1/2 cups flour
1/2 teaspoon salt
1/2 cup vegetable oil
1/4 cup milk

Combine the flour and salt in a medium bowl and blend in the oil, mixing well. Add the milk 1 tablespoon at a time, mixing with a fork until the mixture forms a ball. Chill, wrapped in plastic wrap, for 30 minutes or longer.

Press dough evenly over the bottom and up the side of a 9-inch pie plate and flute the edge. Bake at 350 degrees until golden brown. Cool and fill as desired.

Makes 1 pie shell
Jo Anne Mitchell, Richland Hills Public Library

Elephant Stew

1 elephant
2 cups salt
2 cups pepper
2 rabbits (optional)

Cut the elephant into 1-inch cubes (allow approximately 72 days for this procedure), frequently adding pinches of salt and pepper. Cook over kerosene fire for about 4 weeks at 465 degrees. If more than 3,800 guests are expected for dinner, two rabbits may be added. But do this only if necessary as most people do not like to find hare in their stew.

Serves 3,800
Written by Lucille Brown,
a friend of Brenda Groschup, Haltom City Public Library

Contributors List

Frances Allen, EMS
Lynn Allen, DHJ
Leticia Alviar, SEM
Marsha Anderson, CEN
Sylvia Autrey, WWD
Connie Barnes, WPL
Edith Beightol, Floater
Jill Blake, CEN
Rodney Bland, HCL
Karen Brown, CEN
Wanda Cargill, HCL
Martha Carter, CEN
Laura Cleveland, WPL
Renée Cordray, RDG
Angie Crichett, HCL
Becky Deaton, HCL
Cate Dixon, CEN
Dorothy Douglas, HCL
Marion Edwards, RVS
Dianne Elrod, HCL
Corina Escamilla, WWD
Gena Fisher, CEN
Lynn Frazier, SWTR
Eric Fry, CEN
Barb Grisell, SGN

Brenda Groschup, HCL
Lynne Harmon, CEN
Sarah Harris, RVS
Kathleen Heath, CEN
Max Hill, CEN
Betty Howe, KPL
Tessie Hudson, CEN
Gerry Humphreys, WWD
Pat Jermyn, RHPL
Cheri Jewell, CEN
Betty King, WPL
Brenda Lanche, RVS
Lida Launius, RHPL
Helen Leavell, SWTR
Wynona F. Lee, Floater
Allison Long, HCL
Rina Lutts, HCL
Brenda McCrary, RHPL
Keith Miller, CEN
Pearlie Miller, EBY
Jo Anne Mitchell, RHPL
Cydney Nida, HCL
Anne Noyes, RHPL
Cindy Olson, SWTR
Hilda Olson, CEN

Betty Patterson, RHPL
Cornelia Pim, SEM
Mary Ann Prince, CEN
Raydene Rankin, SWTR
Rebecca Reedy, CEN
Ann Gray Rethard, HCL
Irene Roa, WWD
Gleniece Robinson, CEN
Roberta Schenewerk, CEN
Melva Siddiq, Floater
Mary Taggart Sikes, CEN
Barbara M. Smith, CEN,
    Retired
Deborah Smith, SEM
Lesley Smith, HCL
Doris Snider, HCL
Melissa Speed, CEN
Clark Strickland, EMS
Connie Sullivan, KPL
Arlon Taylor, WWD
Faye Turner, BOLD
Linda Waggener, Floater
Ellen Warthoe, RDG/WWD
Betty Wilson, RHPL
Lisa Harper Wood, KPL

Fort Worth Library Abbreviations

BOLD Butler Outreach Library
CEN Central Library
COOL Cavile Outreach Opportunity Library
DHJ Diamond Hill/Jarvis Branch
EBY East Berry Branch
ESTR East Regional Library
MBK Meadowbrook Branch
NRS Northside Branch

RDG Ridglea Branch
RVS Riverside Branch
SEM Seminary South Branch
EMS Ella Mae Shamblee Branch
SWTR Southwest Regional Library
SGN Summerglen Branch
WWD Wedgwood Branch

MetroPac Libraries

HCL Haltom City Public Library
KPL Keller Public Library

RHPL Richland Hills Public Library
WPL Watauga Public Library

Index